Example-Based Super Resolution

Example-Based Super Resolution

Jordi Salvador

AMSTERDAM • BOSTON • HEIDELBERG • LONDON
NEW YORK • OXFORD • PARIS • SAN DIEGO
SAN FRANCISCO • SINGAPORE • SYDNEY • TOKYO
Academic Press is an imprint of Elsevier

Academic Press is an imprint of Elsevier
125 London Wall, London EC2Y 5AS, United Kingdom
525 B Street, Suite 1800, San Diego, CA 92101-4495, United States
50 Hampshire Street, 5th Floor, Cambridge, MA 02139, United States
The Boulevard, Langford Lane, Kidlington, Oxford OX5 1GB, United Kingdom

Notices
Knowledge and best practice in this field are constantly changing. As new research and experience
broaden our understanding, changes in research methods, professional practices, or medical treatment
may become necessary.

Practitioners and researchers must always rely on their own experience and knowledge in evaluating
and using any information, methods, compounds, or experiments described herein. In using such
information or methods they should be mindful of their own safety and the safety of others, including
parties for whom they have a professional responsibility.

To the fullest extent of the law, neither the Publisher nor the authors, contributors, or editors, assume
any liability for any injury and/or damage to persons or property as a matter of products liability,
negligence or otherwise, or from any use or operation of any methods, products, instructions, or ideas
contained in the material herein.

Library of Congress Cataloging-in-Publication Data
A catalog record for this book is available from the Library of Congress

British Library Cataloguing-in-Publication Data
A catalogue record for this book is available from the British Library

ISBN 978-0-12-809703-8

For information on all Academic Press publications
visit our website at https://www.elsevier.com/

**Working together
to grow libraries in
developing countries**

www.elsevier.com • www.bookaid.org

Publisher: Joe Hayton
Acquisition Editor: Tim Pitts
Editorial Project Manager: Charlotte Kent
Production Project Manager: Kiruthika Govindaraju
Cover Designer: Matthew Limbert

Typeset by SPi Global, India

To my beloved wife, Sibylle,
and my loving parents and sister.

CONTENTS

List of Figures ix

Acknowledgment xi

Introduction xiii

Chapter 1 Classic Multiframe Super Resolution **1**

1.1 Problem Statement 1

1.2 Bayesian Inference 2

1.3 Interpolation-Based Methods 4

1.4 Performance Limits 12

1.5 Discussion 13

Chapter 2 A Taxonomy of Example-Based Super Resolution **15**

2.1 Example-Based Super Resolution 15

2.2 Internal Learning 17

2.3 External Learning 21

2.4 Discussion 28

Chapter 3 High-Frequency Transfer **31**

3.1 Adaptive Filter Selection 31

3.2 Robustness to Aliasing 37

3.3 Robustness to Noise 39

3.4 Discussion 49

Chapter 4 Neighbor Embedding **51**

4.1 Framework 51

4.2 Extensions 56

4.3 Performance 60

4.4 Discussion 62

Chapter 5 Sparse Coding.. **65**

5.1 Super Resolution Model 65

5.2 Adaptive Extension 69

5.3 Application.. 72

5.4 Discussion.. 77

Chapter 6 Anchored Regression **79**

6.1 Anchored Regression Framework 79

6.2 Extensions.. 82

6.3 Performance 88

6.4 Discussion.. 94

Chapter 7 Trees and Forests.. **95**

7.1 Hierarchical Manifold Learning 96

7.2 Naive Bayes Super-Resolution Forest..................................... 101

7.3 Performance 104

7.4 Discussion.. 111

Chapter 8 Deep Learning **113**

8.1 Neural Networks... 113

8.2 Networks for Super Resolution 119

8.3 Performance 124

8.4 Discussion.. 127

Chapter 9 Conclusions **129**

9.1 Overview 129

9.2 Perspective... 132

References 135

LIST OF FIGURES

1   One-dimensional interpolation

2   Sup-pixel shift for multi-frame super resolution

3   Overview of the book structure

1.1   Interpolation-based multi-frame super-resolution pipeline

1.2   Blind deblurring of a synthetically blurred image

1.3   Synthetic example with multi-frame super resolution

1.4   Single-image vs. multi-frame interpolation with compression

1.5   Nearest-neighbor vs. multi-frame interpolation examples

2.1   High-frequency transfer for super resolution

2.2   Neighbor embedding for internal learning

2.3   Sparse coding for super resolution

2.4   Anchored regression for super resolution

2.5   Regression trees for super resolution

2.6   Convolutional networks for super resolution

2.7   Machine learning in the super-resolution taxonomy

3.1   Effects of filter selection

3.2   Spatial distribution of adaptive filter selection

3.3   Histogram of adaptive filter selection

3.4   Filter selection quantitative performance

3.5   Filter selection qualitative performance

3.6   A system with local robustness to aliasing

3.7   Robustness to aliasing with $\times 4$ upscaling

3.8   Robustness to aliasing with $\times 2$ upscaling

3.9   Cross-scale self-similarity robust to noise

3.10   Degradation of SNR after noisy-image super resolution

3.11   Exponential noise decay after downscaling

3.12   Distribution of example scale for different noise levels

3.13   Noise robustness qualitative performance

3.14   Noise robustness quantitative performance

4.1   Neighbor embedding cross-scale geometry preservation

4.2   Polyphase filter in a 1-dimensional case

4.3   Multiphase examples for neighbor embedding

5.1   Sparse reconstruction illustrated

5.2   Adaptive training regions for different input patches

5.3   Sparse coding visual results

6.1   Improved training for anchored neighborhood

6.2   Improved manifold linearization toy example

6.3   Spherical hashing for anchored regression

6.4   Hashing-based speedup for anchored regression

6.5   Qualitative analysis of anchored regression

6.6   Hashing granularity vs. anchored regression performance

7.1   Hierarchical clustering overview

7.2   Manifold span reduction through patch pre-processing

7.3   Unimodal vs. bimodal manifold learning

7.4   Problem of tree selection from an ensemble

7.5   Quantitative performance of forest-based super resolution

7.6   Forest-based super resolution visual results

8.1   Deep learning for Super Resolution

8.2   Multi-layer perceptron

8.3   Back-propagation algorithm for network learning

8.4   Convolutional network motivation

8.5   Neural network design trade-off

8.6   Graphical representation of convolutional networks

8.7   Convolutional network for Super Resolution

8.8   Recursive ISTA algorithm for sparse coding

8.9   Feed-forward LISTA algorithm for deep learning

8.10   LISTA for Super Resolution

ACKNOWLEDGMENT

I would like to thank all the people who I have had the pleasure of working with during the last years, who have passionately discussed every single imaginable aspect about super resolution and machine learning and have definitely been involved, even if indirectly, in the completion of this book. My special thanks go to Eduardo Pérez-Pellitero, who I have had the pleasure of closely supervising during the development of his PhD thesis. He has been an incredible source of ideas and solutions to the visualization of some of the machine-learning concepts that ended up being included in this book. I also want to thank Professor Javier Ruiz-Hidalgo, who, despite the geographic distance, has always been active in our discussions and has, thus, decisively influenced the selection of topics included in the book, and, of course, Professor Bodo Rosenhahn, who has posed countless questions that eventually led to some of the breakthroughs discussed in this book. I would also like to thank Mehmet Türkan, whose contributions to super resolution are absolutely inspiring and whose collaboration in a tutorial on super resolution, co-presented by both of us in Québec, also encouraged me to take the challenge of writing this book. Last, but not least, I cannot finish this acknowledgment without thanking the editorial team at Elsevier for their kindness and willingness to ease the task of preparing the manuscript.

INTRODUCTION

The very first and essential question that a reader might expect a book on super resolution to answer is:

What is super resolution?

The short and direct answer comes from the description of the objective: Given a low-resolution visual input (either a low-resolution image or a set of images, for example, corresponding to frames in a video sequence), estimate the corresponding high-resolution visual output.

THE SUPER-RESOLUTION PROBLEM

The second question that the reader might have is:

When do we need super resolution?

Even though in the last years we have witnessed a progressive increase in the resolution of image and visual sensors, in many applications we might still require higher resolutions than those attainable by available capturing devices (Park, Park, & Kang, 2003). The goals range from providing better content visualization for traditional image processing applications to achieving better visual recognition, including computer vision tasks (Dai, Wang, Chen, & Van Gool, 2016). These requirements apply to diverse fields, such as medical imaging, video surveillance, entertainment, and astronomy, among others.

At least intuitively, it seems clear that having higher resolutions is beneficial for many applications. However, considering the existence of technical alternatives to super resolution, the next question is:

Why do we actually need super resolution?

Let us try to answer this question by first summarizing the main technical limitations in imaging devices and systems:

- The presence of optical distortions and lens blur, typically modeled as the *point spread function*, or PSF.
- Insufficient sensor sampling density and aliasing.
- Motion blur due to low shutter speed.
- The presence of noise due to sensor limitations and also to lossy coding, resulting from transmission and storage constraints.

The way to avoid super resolution would be to ignore the technically achievable vs. economic solution trade-off and attempt to provide devices with excellent spatial (or temporal) resolution, at the cost of a very high market price of the imaging device. Some hardware-related tools to accomplish this include:

- Reducing the pixel size, which unfortunately leads to an increasing appearance of shot noise as the amount of light captured by the device decreases.
- Increasing the chip size to accommodate a larger number of pixel sensors, which unfortunately, results in an increased capacitance.
- Reducing the shutter speed, which leads to an increasing noise level.
- The adoption of high-precision optics and sensors, which invariably results in an increase in the price of the device.

The alternative solution, provided by super resolution, is to use software-related tools in order to obtain the high-resolution visual output. The advantage of postprocessing the captured visual data is that it allows us to trade off computational and hardware costs, which results in systems that, on the one hand, may have a lower market price and, on the other, can work with contemporary imaging devices and systems.

SUPER-RESOLUTION APPROACHES

The next question, and the main one this books attempts to answer during the next chapters, is:

How can we obtain super resolution?

The timeline of approaches for super resolution includes early algorithms based on resampling (interpolation), second generation algorithms based on combining the information from several captures of the same scene (multiframe super resolution), and contemporary algorithms based on machine learning models exploiting available examples (example-based super resolution). Let us briefly summarize their principles.

Interpolation

Not surprisingly, the simplest way to provide super resolution is to apply interpolation on the sampled visual data acquired from the sensor. This approach, which is present, for example, in digital cameras via the digital zoom, ultimately relies on operations based on linear filtering. Thus, it is not possible to obtain high-frequency information in the resized images due to the low-pass behavior of interpolation filters, as illustrated by the one-dimensional example in Fig. 1. Note that, given the spectrum of the signal y sampled with (spatial) frequency f_y and a suitable, ideal interpolation filter, we can only estimate the lower part of the spectrum of the high-resolution version x sampled with frequency $f_x > f_y$ without introducing aliasing artifacts.

This behavior results from the choice of any interpolation filter, including bilinear, bicubic, or Lanczos (windowed sinc function), among others. In all cases, the low-frequency band of the high-resolution image will be more or less accurately reconstructed, with some more noticeable differences around the cutoff frequency and empty high-frequency band. We can also understand the super-resolution problem as that of finding the missing spectral contents of the resampled image. Indeed, filling the empty high-frequency band will produce detailed contents in contrast to the smooth output of interpolation approaches. An advanced super-resolution approach must aim at reconstructing or synthesizing the missing detail, while ensuring a clear visual output consistent with the observed visual input.

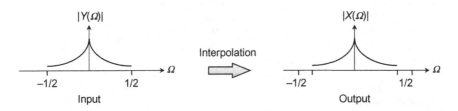

Fig. 1 One-dimensional interpolation example. Given y sampled at frequency f_y, represented by the magnitude of its discrete Fourier transform Y vs. its normalized frequency $\Omega = f/f_y$, the application of an ideal interpolation filter to obtain a resampled version x at frequency $f_x > f_y$ results in a low-pass signal with the normalized frequency $\Omega = f/f_x$.

Multiframe Super Resolution

The first alternative is to combine the information contained on multiple low-resolution captures of the same scene to estimate the high-resolution visual output. The advantage of this approach is that, given an accurate registration of the low-resolution captures, the missing detail in each of them can be (partially) reconstructed if the sampling points are such that subpixel shifts appear between low-resolution capture pairs, as illustrated in Fig. 2. This follows the intuition that super resolution from multiple captures should work when the available images do provide complementary information about the scene.

Many different approaches exist for combining multiframe captures for super resolution, which can be coarsely classified into frequency-domain methods, Bayesian inference methods, or interpolation-based methods. The latter should not be confused with the single-image interpolation upscaling described above. Unfortunately, the performance of these approaches is

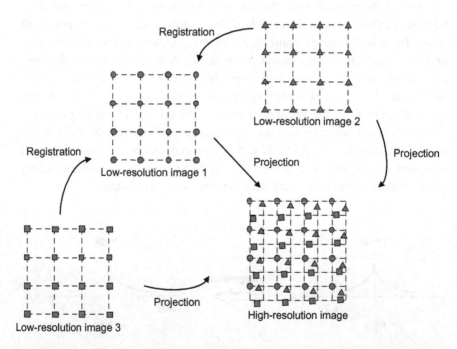

Fig. 2 *Multiframe super resolution only works when low-resolution images provide different sampling points of the scene. In this example, two additional images are registered to the pose of image 1 and the information of all three images is combined by projection onto a high-resolution grid. It would not be possible to gain complementary information to fill in the gaps in the high-resolution grid if there would only exist an integer translational shift between the low-resolution images.*

fundamentally limited by registration accuracy in real-world scenarios. The registration accuracy, in turn, is affected by the effects of blur and noise, apart from the characteristics of the scene itself (amount of texture and structure). In practice, the resolution gain that can be expected from multiframe super-resolution is unfortunately low, so more robust techniques are required for providing higher resolutions.

Example-Based Super Resolution
The second, and arguably most successful, alternative is to estimate the high-resolution version of an image by exploiting examples. In a very naïve example, imagine we are given a low-resolution landscape with the lower part of the picture showing the sea and the upper part, blue sky with some clouds. If we have a database of high-resolution sea and sky images, which we can, for example, downscale to the resolution of our visual input, we can look for the low-resolution examples that best resemble the two parts of our given image and reconstruct the high-resolution version with a montage of the sky and sea high-resolution parts. Of course, successful example-based, super-resolution approaches should be generalizable, which can be typically achieved by dividing images into small (overlapping) patches.

The latest advances on this super-resolution strategy, based on different flavors of machine learning, can be classified as internal-learning and external-learning methods. The evolution and advantages of all methods lying in these categories are the main focus of this book, and will be thoroughly discussed throughout the next chapters. For now, let us briefly justify the success of this strategy based on two facts. The first one is that the numerical limitations of registration accuracy in multiframe super resolution allow only for limited resolution gains in most real-world scenarios. The second one is the data-driven momentum of signal processing and statistics. The large amounts of data and computational power allow us to exploit machine learning algorithms to learn patterns and models to provide an accuracy level that traditional parametric models cannot rival. The power of nonparametric, machine-learned models has thus, a positive impact, not only for super-resolution applications, but also for other imaging and computer vision problems.

OUTLINE

The rest of this book provides a short overview of classic multiframe super resolution and its limiting factors and a detailed, yet compact, description of the two main classes of example-based super resolution from a machine-learning perspective. A graphical representation of the structure of the book is shown in Fig. 3.

- In Chapters 1 and 2 we review the imaging model, reconstruction techniques, and pitfalls of classic super resolution from multiple captures, followed by a general classification of example-based super-resolution techniques as either belonging to internal or external learning methods.
- In Chapters 3 and 4 we describe the two most relevant approaches in internal learning-based super resolution, that is, high-frequency transfer and neighbor embedding (which can also be applied with external learning) for cross-scale self-similarity. Internal learning is especially suitable in scenarios where offline training is not an option.
- In Chapters 5 through 8 we describe the most relevant models for external learning-based super resolution, including sparse coding, anchored regression, regression trees and forests and, finally, deep learning. These algorithms provide state-of-the-art performance when appropriate training data are available during an offline stage.
- In Chapter 9 we overview the achievements and limits of state-of-the-art approaches in example-based super resolution and discuss open challenges and future lines of research.

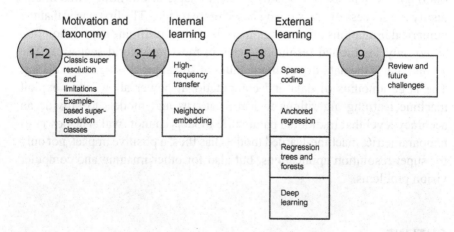

Fig. 3 *The book can be divided into four groups of chapters. The first group justifies and provides a classification of existing example-based methods; the second group presents methods based on internal learning; the third group presents methods based on external learning, and the final chapter provides an overview and presents some challenges for upcoming applications.*

About the Book

Image processing and computer vision are topics covered by many excellent books. Most known (and yet unknown) algorithms can be devised from the hints offered by their authors by conveniently adapting the working principles of their described methods and models to the specific requirements of each application. The main goal of this book is to complement those references in order to provide the reader with a compact description of the most relevant insights of the latest and most successful approaches in super resolution. Whereas this goal is primarily targeted at researchers and developers directly working on super resolution, the book still attempts to provide a sufficiently complete description of contemporary, powerful, and general image models that can also be applied to other image processing and computer vision problems. Last, but not least, the book can also be used as a survey of machine learning models applied to regression applications, which might make it a useful resource even for other signal processing or statistical problems not specifically dealing with image data.

CHAPTER 1

Classic Multiframe Super Resolution

In contrast to the ideas presented throughout the rest of the book, this chapter introduces and discusses classic approaches in super resolution, which attempt to provide a finer sampling of a visual scene by combining several coarse and, possibly corrupted, captures. We shall start by defining a suitable model to describe the problem and the available solutions, and later discuss the shortcomings of these approaches.

1.1 PROBLEM STATEMENT

Let Y be a low-resolution (i.e., subsampled) and corrupted version of a desired image X for which we cannot directly obtain a capture with sufficient spatial resolution:

$$Y(u, v) = X(u + \Delta u, v + \Delta v) * H \downarrow s + N(u, v), \qquad (1.1)$$

where u and v denote any pixel location in rows and columns, respectively, s is the subsampling factor of the observed image Y with respect to the desired image X, H is a certain low-pass function attempting to prevent aliasing from appearing in Y, Δu and Δv represent the optical flow (horizontal and vertical displacement, respectively) between X and Y, and N is additive, independent noise.

Let us now assume that we can obtain an arbitrarily large number N_I of subsampled and corrupted images, each with a different displacement or optical flow with respect to the desired image:

$$Y_i(u, v) = X(u + \Delta u_i, v + \Delta v_i) * H \downarrow s + N_i(u, v), \quad i = 1, \ldots N_I. \quad (1.2)$$

Note that we assume the same low-pass filter or blur function H for all observed images. Even though this notation cannot handle all the possible cases, it will be difficult (and costly) to determine the blur function in a frame-by-frame basis, so this formula does actually describe the most common scenario.

1.1.1 A Frequency-Domain Pipeline

Early efforts in super resolution from multiple images focused on frequency-domain approaches. The main idea is to enhance details by extrapolating

Example-Based Super Resolution. http://dx.doi.org/10.1016/B978-0-12-809703-8.00001-0

the high-frequency information of the available images with a relatively low computational complexity through (the use of fast Fourier transforms) under the additional assumption of global translational motion, which further constrains target scenarios. The general idea in T. S. Huang and Tsai (1984), S. P. Kim, Bose, and Valenzuela (1990), Tom, Katsaggelos, and Galatsanos (1994), and Vandewalle, Süsstrunk, and Vetterli (2006), among others, is:

1. Transform the low-resolution images to frequency domain using the fast Fourier or wavelet transforms.
2. Combine the transformed images (including registration, blind deconvolution, and interpolation tasks) using Expectation-Maximization algorithms (Dempster, Laird, & Rubin, 1977; Gupta & Chen, 2011).
3. Invert the Fourier or wavelet transform to obtain the reconstructed high-resolution image.

The constraint of global translational motion is unaffordable for most application scenarios (think about video with parallax or, even worse, nonrigid motion), so in the following we reduce the constraints to the earlier mentioned constant blur function for all frames.

1.2 BAYESIAN INFERENCE

Considering that the information extracted from the input images $\{Y_i\}$ reflects the probability distribution of the unknown high-resolution image X and that the observations are independent, we can adopt Bayesian inference to solve the problem of estimating X given $\{Y_i\}$.

1.2.1 Maximum Likelihood

Without exploiting any prior information about the desired image X, the Maximum Likelihood (ML) solution to the super-resolution problem would be

$$\hat{X}_{\mathrm{ML}} = \arg\max_{X} p(\{Y_i\}|X), \tag{1.3}$$

which, assuming independence of observations based on the nature of the noise process, turns into

$$\hat{X}_{\mathrm{ML}} = \arg\max_{X} \prod_i p(Y_i|X). \tag{1.4}$$

Taking Eq. (1.2) into account, the ML estimate of X is

$$\hat{X}_{\mathrm{ML}}(u, v) = \underset{X(u,v)}{\arg\min} \sum_{i=1}^{N_I} \| Y_i(u, v) - X(u + \Delta u_i, v + \Delta v_i) * H \downarrow s \|_2^2,$$

(1.5)

where we assume that Δu_i, Δv_i, and H are known and also that the noise is Gaussian. Note that the optimization with respect to X is linear and allows a closed-form solution. We can also consider an alternative solution where each Y_i is back-warped to the reference pose of the desired image X:

$$\hat{X}_{\mathrm{ML}}(u, v) = \underset{X(u,v)}{\arg\min} \sum_{i=1}^{N_I} \| Y_i(u - \Delta u_i, v - \Delta v_i) - X(u, v) * H \downarrow s \|_2^2.$$

(1.6)

The main shortcoming of the ML solution is that we cannot control its behavior for output pixels for which no observations are available.

1.2.2 Maximum A Posteriori

It is also possible to further extend the robustness of the solution by incorporating prior knowledge about X:

$$\hat{X}_{\mathrm{MAP}} = \underset{X}{\arg\max}\, p(X|\{Y_i\}) = \underset{X}{\arg\max}\, p(\{Y_i\}|X) p(X). \qquad (1.7)$$

Under the same assumptions of observation independence and Gaussian noise as in ML, the Maximum A Posterior (MAP) estimate contains the addition of regularizing constraints:

$$\hat{X}_{\mathrm{MAP}} = \underset{X}{\arg\min} \sum_{i=1}^{N_I} \| Y_i(u - \Delta u_i, v - \Delta v_i) - X * H \downarrow s \|_2^2 + \lambda \mathcal{R}(X),$$

(1.8)

where $\mathcal{R}(X)$ is a regularization function (with a limiting effect on high-frequency energy) on X and λ is a regularization constant or weight. We can safely drop the pixel indices in X for the sake of clarity.

The simplest possible assumption about X is that it should be smooth. Smoothness can be enforced, for example, by imposing Tikhonov regularization (Tikhonov & Arsenin, 1977), which results in the Gaussian Markov Random Field

$$\hat{X}_{\mathrm{Smooth}} = \underset{X}{\arg\min} \sum_{i=1}^{N_I} \| Y_i(u - \Delta u_i, v - \Delta v_i) - X * H \downarrow s \|_2^2 + \lambda \| \nabla X \|_2^2,$$

(1.9)

where λ depends on both the noise level and the statistical distribution of the prior on the gradients, and ∇ acts as a high-pass operator that computes both horizontal and vertical gradients. A nice feature of this estimate is that it again provides a closed form solution on X. However, a smooth gradient assumption does not represent most natural images very well.

By assuming a Laplacian gradients distribution, which better resembles natural image statistics, as shown by Rudin, Osher, and Fatemi (1992) and Eggermont (1993), among others, we can obtain a MAP solution by means of the isotropic form of the Total Variation (TV) regularization constraint:

$$\hat{X}_{\text{TV}} = \arg\min_{X} \sum_{i=1}^{N_I} \|Y_i(u - \Delta u_i, v - \Delta v_i) - X * H \downarrow s\|_2^2 + \lambda \|\nabla X\|_2,$$

(1.10)

Note that a similar solution can be obtained with the anisotropic TV regularization term $\|\nabla X\|_1$, and also that the presence of this regularization term enforces an iterative solution (Chambolle, 2004).

Further MAP estimates can be obtained by, for example, Bilateral TV regularization (Farsiu, Robinson, Elad, & Milanfar, 2004), which uses several scales of derivatives to provide more robust estimates, by Maximum Entropy regularization, commonly used in astronomical imaging (Pantin & Starck, 1996), or even other priors (Elad & Datsenko, 2009).

1.3 INTERPOLATION-BASED METHODS

The multiframe super-resolution problem can also be described as a cascaded combination of several classic image processing subproblems as illustrated in Fig. 1.1. The global problem is thus converted into a concatenation of smaller subproblems. This was already partially done in the Bayesian

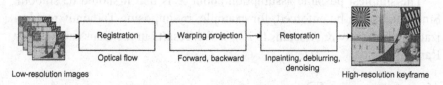

Fig. 1.1 Multiframe super resolution as a concatenation of registration (typically solved via computation of the optical flow), warping projection (which can be computed forward or backward), and restoration (including inpainting in case of using forward warping, deblurring, and denoising).

inference strategies described above, where the computation of the registration was left apart. The new list of problems can be summarized as:

1. **Registration**, which can be solved via the computation of the optical flow between the reference pose (e.g., the one corresponding to the central frame in a video sequence).
2. **Warping projection**, which can be computed forward (possibly leaving gaps) or backward (possibly oversmoothing the output) to combine the information from the available low-resolution images into a high-resolution grid.
3. **Restoration**, which typically consists of a small scale inpainting stage (in case of using forward warping), and a concatenation or combination of deblurring and denoising.

1.3.1 Registration

The problem of registration can be solved by means of computing the motion, subpixel shift, or rotation (described as the dene field $\{\Delta u_i, \Delta v_i\}$) between the reference low-resolution image, that is, the one to be upscaled, and each of the other available images in the sequence. The problem is relatively simple if the motion of the scene is at least approximately fronto-parallel to the camera plane and uniform over the entire scene. Such scenarios might appear, for example, when a flat object projects onto the image plane and moves along a fronto-parallel direction with respect to the image plane, but more interestingly, also when the camera is placed very far away from the scene, such that the scene appears practically flat in the image. In such scenarios, it is possible to adopt frequency-domain approaches based on correlation of the Fourier transform.

Many early works in multiframe super resolution rely on classical *optical flow* estimation techniques with differential equations (like the coarse-to-fine pyramidal approximation based on Lucas & Kanade, 1981 and the regularized improvement by Horn & Schunck, 1981) in order to register the low-resolution images with subpixel precision. More recently, the frequency-domain modeling of rigid transforms has also been revisited by Vandewalle et al. (2006) to tackle problems with rigid motion, but in general, these approaches are not suitable for video sequences with complex nonrigid motion.

Fortunately, recent advances in optical flow estimation manage to provide subpixel accuracy even in the presence of fairly complex motion, as shown in D. Sun, Roth, and Black (2010) and Baker et al. (2011), essentially exploiting nonlocal regularization as a generalization of median filtering for outlier rejection on a model stemming from Horn and Schunck (1981). Even for rigid camera motion, contemporary optical flow methods can improve accuracy with respect to classical approaches. As motion becomes more complex, contemporary methods clearly outperform classical ones, thanks to a greatly reduced amount of outliers. More recent methods progressively allow reducing the amount of outliers in more cases, thanks to the edge-preserving fusion of sparse feature-based matches with the continuous flow field as in the recent work by Revaud, Weinzaepfel, Harchaoui, and Schmid (2015). In general, simpler (and faster) block matching techniques do not suffice to accurately describe the subpixel motion between frames, although some ways to improve the accuracy based on iterative refinement of the matches can provide reasonable approximations of the optical flow fields (Salvador, Kochale, & Schweidler, 2013).

As we shall see below, the computation of the motion vectors from each low-resolution frame toward the low-resolution keyframe results in a natural application of forward warping when fusing the information from all the available images. The alternative, backward warping, involves the computation of the motion vectors from an interpolation-based upscaled version of the keyframe to the additional interpolated versions of the other high-resolution images, which naturally results in a higher computational cost in both terms of time and space complexity.

1.3.2 Warping Projection

The next step is to warp all available low-resolution frames using the registration data or motion vectors in order to fill in an initially empty high-resolution grid corresponding to the sampling positions of the high-resolution version of the keyframe, that is, with the same number of pixels as the desired high-resolution image. There are two general ways to accomplish this, regarding the motion vectors used: forward warping (vectors from each frame to the keyframe) or backward warping (vectors from interpolated estimates of the high-resolution keyframe to each frame). In this section, we use the bilinearly weighted nearest neighbors interpolation, but nonuniform interpolation, or wavelet-based interpolation can also be used.

Forward Warping

For each low-resolution image Y_i with registration $(\Delta u_i, \Delta v_i)$, upscaling factor s, and uniformly sampled positions (u, v), we compute target warped positions for each image as

$$(u'_i, v'_i) = (su + s\Delta u_i, sv + s\Delta v_i),\tag{1.11}$$

which in general are noninteger positions (u'_i, v'_i). Thus, the contribution to each of the four closest pixels in the high-resolution grid around each warped position are modulated by bilinear weights regarding their proximities to the computed position (e.g., $(u' - \lfloor u' \rfloor)(v' - \lfloor v' \rfloor)$ for the nearest bottom right pixels corresponding to each warped position). After accumulating the contributions from all N_I warped frames, the resulting high-resolution grid must be normalized by the accumulated weights. A binary mask M can also be obtained, indicating which pixels in the high-resolution grid have not received any contribution from the warped frames, for the subsequent restoration stage.

Backward Warping

The alternative to avoid gaps in the high-resolution grid is to use backward warping. In this case, we start from uniformly sampled positions over the high-resolution grid (u, v). For each interpolated image Y_i with backward registration $(\Delta u_i, \Delta v_i)$ and upscaling factor s, we compute the corresponding low-resolution positions

$$(u'_i, v'_i) = (u/s + \Delta u_i/s, v/s + \Delta v_i/s),\tag{1.12}$$

which in general will result in noninteger positions (u'_i, v'_i) for each neighbor frame. Thus, the contribution from each of the four closest pixels in the low-resolution grid around each backward-warped position can be modulated by bilinear weights regarding their proximity to the computed position (e.g., $(1 - (u' - \lfloor u' \rfloor))(1 - (v' - \lfloor v' \rfloor))$ for the nearest top left pixels corresponding to each warped position). After accumulating the contributions from all warped N_I frames, the resulting high-resolution grid must be normalized by the accumulated weights. Obviously, at the end of this procedure there are no gaps in the HR grid, but the result tends to look oversmoothed when compared to the one obtained by forward warping.

1.3.3 Restoration

The image resulting from the fusion procedure ensuing from registration and warping projection contains a richer amount of detail than any of the individual single frames employed, but potentially has the problem of containing a substantial amount of blur and additive noise, apart from the presence of gaps due to forward warping. The techniques presented in this section aim at enhancing the output image by small-scale inpainting, deblurring, and denoising.

Inpainting

We have already seen that, when using forward warping, some of the pixels in the high-resolution grid can be empty. In order to fill in these gaps, a small-scale inpainting approach can be added during the restoration stage. A simple small-scale inpainter can be formulated as an initialization $X_b := X_0$, where X_0 is the image resulting from warping projection, and a constrained optimization

$$\hat{X}_b := \min_{X_b} \mathcal{R}(X_b), \quad \text{s.t. } X_b(u, v) = X_0(u, v) \quad \forall (u, v)|M(u, v) = 0,$$

$$(1.13)$$

where the subindex b stands for blurry and the mask M, obtained during the warping projection stage, equals one for initially empty pixels and zero otherwise. $\mathcal{R}$ is a regularizer reflecting a priori knowledge about the image statistics. For example, assuming a smooth image model, a Tikhonov regularizer can be adopted. The corresponding solution using gradient descent is

$$X_b^{(t+1)} := X_b^{(t)} - \mu M(\Delta X_b^{(t)}),$$

$$(1.14)$$

where μ is a constant update step, Δ is the Laplacian operator and, abusing notation, $M(\cdot)$ outputs the input when $M = 1$ and 0, otherwise. This approach for small-scale inpanting implicitly assumes noiseless pixels (noise is treated in a subsequent stage). It is also possible to combine inpainting and denoising with a slightly more involved variational formulation, including a data term and a different regularization scheme like the costly total curvature (Goldluecke & Cremers, 2011).

Deblurring

Blind deblurring (deblurring with unknown blur kernel) is a well-known problem, that is, best solved by first estimating the blur kernel or Point Spread Function (PSF) and then applying nonblind deblurring, that is, deblurring with known PSF, because the asymmetry between the (small) number of unknowns and a reasonable number of available pixels, when attempting to estimate the blur kernel (PSF) separately from deblurring the image is beneficial (Joshi, Szeliski, & Kriegman, 2008). The estimation of the PSF also benefits from the choice of a linear regularizer in the previous processing stages, for a linear (invariant) process can be conveniently described by means of a convolution kernel. This would not hold with, for example, TV regularization, which would require more complex deblurring techniques (Takeda, Farsiu, & Milanfar, 2008).

In order to estimate the PSF, we can follow an edge-based approach akin to the one described by Joshi et al. (2008). First, an estimate of the sharp pixels around the salient edges in the high-resolution image can be obtained by:

1. Canny edge detection on the fused (inpainted) high-resolution image;
2. Edge-transversal local binarization (to the maximum and minimum pixel values at each side of the edge).
3. Linear transition of pixel values between the positions of the two extrema.

Once the image with sharp transitions around salient edges, which we can name X_d, has been estimated by this method, it can be used for estimating the PSF in closed-form (possible by using a Tikhonov regularizer) or with a gradient descent approach, as in Joshi et al. (2008). For the sake of readability, in the following we avoid referring to indicator functions (masks) for estimated sharp pixels in the neighborhood of salient edges. Let H be the PSF to be estimated, X_b the (still blurry) super-resolution image, and $\mathcal{R}(H)$ a Tikhonov regularizer for PSF smoothness. We look for

$$\hat{H} := \min_{H} \| X_b - X_d * H \|_2^2 + \lambda_H \mathcal{R}(H), \qquad (1.15)$$

which accepts an efficient closed-form solution for the estimation of the PSF.

Once the shape of the PSF is known, we can marginalize on the other unknown of the blur model

$$\hat{X}_n := \min_{X_n} \| X_b - X_n * H \|_2^2 + \lambda_d \mathcal{R}(X_n), \qquad (1.16)$$

where λ_d is a small regularization factor included for numerical stability, $\mathcal{R}(x_n)$ is a Tikhonov regularizer, and the subindex n stands for noisy. By using this type of regularizer (which has minimal influence on the result, especially with a small noise level), we can once again obtain a closed-form solution. A visual comparison of a synthetically blurry and noisy image and the deblurred output obtained with this blind deblurring procedure is shown in Fig. 1.2.

Denoising

In contrast to deblurring, the choice of the regularizer has a clear impact on the results obtained when denoising, especially with high noise levels.

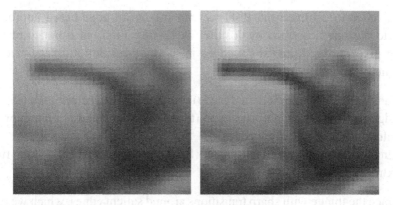

Fig. 1.2 Close-up of a blind deblurring experiment on a synthetically blurred image. Left, input blurred and slightly noisy image; right, deblurred image via estimation of the PSF based on a sharp edge assumption and Tikhonov-regularized deblurring.

TV is a powerful regularizer for this task (Rudin et al., 1992). The resulting formulation under the assumption of Gaussian noise is

$$\hat{X} := \min_X \|X_n - X\|_2^2 + \lambda_f \mathcal{R}(X) \qquad (1.17)$$

with $\mathcal{R}(X)$ any of the anisotropic or isotropic TV regularizers. The practical consequence of using a TV regularizer is the impossibility of obtaining a closed-form solution. Possible iterative solutions include the Iteratively Reweighted Least Squares method (Green, 1984) or Chambolle's projection algorithm (Chambolle, 2004).

Iterative Reconstruction
It is also possible to combine the projection and restoration stages in a single process to obtain a simultaneous solution. For example, the Projection Onto Convex Sets (POCS) framework originally presented by Stark and Oskoui (1989) provides constrained solution sets with a prior image model. Alternatively, the Iterative Back-Projection (IBP) algorithm by Irani and Peleg (1990) iteratively projects and cancels the error from the low-resolution.

Some sample results for multiframe super resolution from synthetic video sequences with relatively large upscaling factors ($s = 4$) are shown in Fig. 1.3. A sample result from a real-world scenario with compressed video and a more conservative upscaling factor ($s = 2$) is also shown in Fig. 1.4. In Fig. 1.5, sample results from standard (noisy) sequences without compression artifacts for $s = 4$ are shown. In all cases it is clear that the level

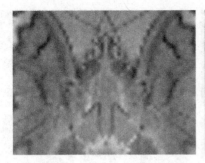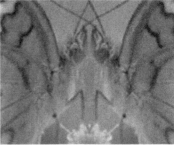

Fig. 1.3 Comparison of synthetic video upscaling with s = 4. Left, upscaled image obtained via bicubic interpolation (single-image) corresponding to the reference frame of the video sequence; right, upscaled reference frame obtained with multiframe interpolation-based super resolution.

Fig. 1.4 Detail of super-resolution upscaling with s = 2 using bicubic interpolation (right) and multiframe interpolation-based super resolution method (left) for a lossy compressed video sequence.

of detail of the multiframe super-resolved images is higher than that of the respective input images, and also higher than the single-image interpolation counterparts. However, it is also true that the reconstructed images are not as sharp as native images in the target resolutions. This behavior can be observed, for example, by perceiving that the transitions around the sharpest edges in the reconstructed images still span over several pixels.

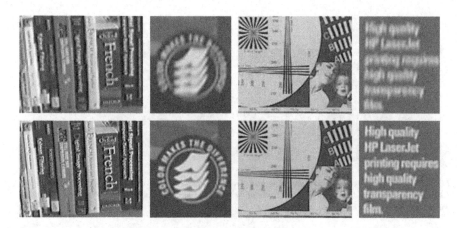

Fig. 1.5 Examples of interpolation-based multiframe super resolution with 4× upscaling with noisy video sequences. The top row shows the single-image nearest-neighbor interpolation of the reference frame in each video sequence; the bottom row shows the super-resolution result for the same frames.

Further methods combining registration, warping projection, and restoration into a joint solution have also been explored by Pickup, Capel, Roberts, and Zisserman (2007) and C. Liu and Sun (2014). These methods adapt the principles behind Bayesian inference to the specific requirements in each super-resolution task (registration, projection, and restoration) described in this section.

1.4 PERFORMANCE LIMITS

Using ground-truth data (synthetic subpixel-shifted image sequences), as in Fig. 1.3, we can subjectively and quantitatively assess that multiframe super-resolution provides better accuracy than single-image interpolation. Indeed, averaging the results in a larger collection of examples, including the mentioned one, the SSIM (structural similarity) index and Y-PSNR (luminance Peak Signal to Noise Ratio) are 0.45 and 18.09 dB for bicubic interpolation and 0.74 and 22.47 dB for multiframe super-resolution, respectively.

In the example with low-quality compressed video in Fig. 1.4, we can also see how multiframe super-resolution is capable of retrieving more detail than single-image interpolation for smaller upscaling factors ($s = 2$), but the resolution gain appears naturally more limited than, for example, the ones shown in Fig. 1.5, where the video sequences are corrupted by less noticeable additive Gaussian noise.

Naturally, the performance is sensitive to the registration accuracy, which decays as the motion becomes highly nonuniform and rapid. Indeed, the main limiting factors of reconstruction-based SR are errors due to inaccurate image registration, followed by the impact of errors in the estimation of the PSF. Registration is still an open challenge for most video sequences with nonrigid and complex motion, and it also degrades fast whenever the magnification factor is large, or the number of available images is insufficient, as shown by Baker and Kanade (2002) and Z. Lin and Shum (2004).

In practice, even with a rather strong constraint, such as local translation, which does not take into account the effect of nonuniform motion, the numerical stability issues for registration and errors in PSF estimation result in an effective upscaling factor bounded by $s = 1.6$ which, only under synthetic considerations, could reach a higher limit of $s = 5.7$, as deduced by Z. Lin and Shum (2004). Attempting to go beyond these factors will lead to either grid-like artifacts due to the wrong registration or oversmoothing. There is also a boundary on the minimal number of available low-resolution images, which further limits the applicability for general video sequences with complex motion. In conclusion, it is necessary to develop alternative algorithms to achieve large effective upscaling factors in general scenarios.

1.5 DISCUSSION

Multiframe super resolution has been a very active research topic during the last decades (Farsiu, Robinson, Elad, & Milanfar, 2003; Irani & Peleg, 1990; C. Liu & Sun, 2014; Tsai & Huang, 1984), and interest in this family of super-resolution methods is still high due to the fact that, in the presence of notable aliasing and noise, robust reconstruction-based techniques (Farsiu et al., 2003) can be better suited than other alternatives.

In this chapter we have formulated the multiframe super-resolution problem and discussed different alternatives for solving it, with special focus on Bayesian inference strategies and the more analytical interpolation-based multiframe super-resolution strategy. However, the visual results reflect a limited effective resolution gain that has also been theoretically justified. Alternative methods based on exploiting defocus or zoom cues have also been described by Chaudhuri and Manjunath (2005). Even though these alternatives can alleviate the registration accuracy challenges, their use is not generalizable to general images and videos.

The rest of the book focuses on the alternative family of example-based super-resolution methods based on machine learning. As we shall see, machine learning provides several techniques that effectively enable the robust application of large upscaling factors with general applicability. The multiframe super-resolution methods presented in this chapter can also be used as input or initialization for the subsequent example-based methods when more than one low-resolution input frame is available.

CHAPTER 2

A Taxonomy of Example-Based Super Resolution

Before starting the detailed description of the most powerful machine learning approaches for example-based super resolution, it is worth spending some time exploring the similarities and differences between them. This comparative review leads to a hierarchical classification, illustrated in Fig. 2.7, of the methods that are analyzed in the next chapters.

2.1 EXAMPLE-BASED SUPER RESOLUTION

Without the availability of multiframe visual inputs, the example-based super-resolution problem is simplified to that of estimating a high-resolution version X of a single low-resolution observed image Y, generated by the model

$$Y = (X * H) \downarrow s, \tag{2.1}$$

where $*$ denotes image convolution, H is a filter preventing aliasing from appearing in Y, and $\downarrow s$ is a downsampling operator with scaling factor s (i.e., the desired upscaling factor). A common assumption in the example-based super-resolution literature is that H does not introduce additional blur in Y, so the latter can often be assumed to be sharp. In Michaeli and Irani (2013), a method is proposed, based on internal learning, to estimate the overall blur kernel for super-resolving blurred images, but in the following we keep the no-blur assumption used by most current methods.

Example-based super resolution can be regarded as the broadest classification of the currently most successful alternatives to multiframe super-resolution. The main reason for the success of example-based super resolution can be attributed to the improved generalization of most visual inputs. We must note that, in contrast to multi-frame methods, example-based super resolution aims at hallucinating the missing detail, rather than reconstructing it. Even if in some scenarios it may be convenient to combine the best of both strategies, for example, as shown by Bätz, Eichenseer, Seiler, Jonscher, and Kaup (2015), the rest of the book focuses

Example-Based Super Resolution. http://dx.doi.org/10.1016/B978-0-12-809703-8.00002-2

on the independent application of example-based super resolution. In this section we start by discussing of the differences between parametric and nonparametric example-based methods.

2.1.1 Parametric Methods

Parametric super-resolution methods model the super-resolution problem with mapping functions that are controlled by a relatively compact amount of parameters. These parameters are, in turn, learned from examples that do not necessarily come from the input image.

One possibility is to adapt the interpolation process to the local covariance of the image. The main idea behind algorithms following the natural-image edge-directed interpolation (NEDI) principle (Li & Orchard, 2001) is to first estimate local covariance parameters from a low-resolution image and then use these parameters to adapt the interpolation at a higher resolution, based on a geometric correspondence between the low-resolution and the high-resolution covariances.

We can also learn parametric edge models and impose them on the super-resolved image, as proposed by Fattal (2007). This method is based on a statistical relation of edge features across different resolutions in natural images. Because the output image must also remain similar to the input image after downsampling to the original resolution (back-projection constraint), a constrained optimization problem appears, combining the parametric edge regularization and the imposition of back-projection similarity.

Parametric models are comparatively more powerful than nonparametric ones in terms of efficiency (i.e., less data are needed to estimate the models), and can also provide an easier interpretation of results. However, nonparametric models have the very desirable property of making fewer assumptions. This property, combined with availability of large amounts of training examples and the current computational power for offline training (e.g., cloud, clusters, GPU), makes nonparametric methods a more attractive option.

2.1.2 Nonparametric Methods

Nonparametric models differ from parametric models in that the model structure is not specified a priori, but is instead greatly determined directly from the available training data. The term nonparametric does not imply that they completely lack parameters, but rather that the number and nature of the parameters are flexible and can depend on the training data.

The first aspect to note in nonparametric methods is that input images are decomposed into overlapping patches, and the reconstructed image is obtained by combining the contributions of the computed overlapping output patches. Thus, both the output image X and the input image Y can be treated as sets of overlapping patches $\{x\}$ and $\{y\}$.

Ongoing research on nonparametric methods has recently provided large performance improvements in terms of accuracy and efficiency, thanks to the introduction of the latest machine learning approaches. Some of these methods allow regressing the high-resolution output from just a single visual input (Freeman, Pasztor, & Carmichael, 2000; Glasner, Bagon, & Irani, 2009). Some others can also exploit knowledge gained from external datasets, not necessarily related to the input image (Timofte, De Smet, & Van Gool, 2013; J. Yang, Wright, Huang, & Ma, 2010), which leads to the classification into the internal and external learning approaches that follow.

2.2 INTERNAL LEARNING

The main idea behind methods in this category, as reflected by the name, is that patch examples are obtained directly from the input image, exploiting the cross-scale self-similarity property of natural images (Bevilacqua, Roumy, Guillemot, & Alberi-Morel, 2012; Glasner et al., 2009). This property states that most small patches (e.g., 3×3 pixels) in a natural image are very likely to be found in downscaled versions of the same image. This idea can also be applied to other related problems such as blur kernel estimation (Michaeli & Irani, 2013), denoising (Zontak, Mosseri, & Irani, 2013), and even spatio-temporal video super-resolution (Shahar, Faktor, & Irani, 2011).

Despite the nice properties of these methods, including, for example, their implicit adaptivity to the image contents, an important practical drawback is the computational cost induced by the required nearest-neighbor search. In order to alleviate this problem, one possibility is to exploit the latest and efficient approximate nearest-neighbor search algorithms (Barnes, Shechtman, Finkelstein, & Goldman, 2009; He & Sun, 2012;

Heo, Lee, He, Chang, & Yoon, 2012; Korman & Avidan, 2011; Torres, Salvador, & Pérez-Pellitero, 2014). The alternative is the progressive reduction of the search range for similar patches presented by some of the latest best performing internal learning methods (Freedman & Fattal, 2011; J. Yang, Lin, & Cohen, 2013). The evolution from the work by Glasner et al. (2009) to that of J. Yang et al. (2013) is remarkable. The search on the entire multiscale pyramid of each intermediate image toward the desired scale in the former is reduced to an iterated in-place example selection (one of just nine possible patches in the immediately lower scale) in the latter, thanks to the incorporation of additional prior knowledge from offline training.

Internal learning methods can also be robust to noise. The goal is to obtain better upscaling results (including sharper edges and better preservation of texture) than those obtained by following the standard pipeline of first denoising the input image and then performing upscaling on the denoised image. In Salvador, Pérez-Pellitero, and Kochale (2014), a framework based on cross-scale self-similarity for noisy patches, which takes into account the energy of noise in each scale (Zontak et al., 2013), allows joint upscaling and denoising based entirely on localized multiscale self-examples. A powerful (and costlier) alternative is to perform super resolution from both the noisy and the denoised images, and then perform a convex combination based on spatial (local variance), spectral (band selective mixing), and global (assuming Gaussian additive noise) constraints (Singh, Porikli, & Ahuja, 2014).

For offline applications, where runtime is not a constraint, Cui, Chang, Shan, Zhong, and Chen (2014) propose an iterative fusion of cross-scale self-similarity priors with a collaborative ensemble of patch-level auto-encoder networks to gradually upscale low-resolution images layer by layer, each layer with a small scale factor. The advantage is a better reconstruction of texture in comparison to internal learning approaches. Alternatively, J. B. Huang, Singh, and Ahuja (2015) propose to search over the entire set of pyramidal downscaled versions of an image, extending the search space to include homographic transformations with a generalized Patch-Match approximate nearest-neighbor search scheme (Barnes, Shechtman, Goldman, & Finkelstein, 2010). The idea is to exploit examples even if they do not appear in the same orientation as the current patch. The shortcomings are naturally the higher runtime, and also the limited high-frequency gain from transformed examples due to the effect of interpolation.

2.2.1 High-Frequency Transfer

The general idea behind high-frequency transfer methods is shown in Fig. 2.1. Using interpolation, a coarse version of the super-resolved image can be easily obtained. Since this coarse version lacks high-frequency components, we can exploit cross-scale self-similarity by computing the coarse version of the input image. The difference between the original input image and its coarse version is precisely the high-frequency band that we need to transfer to the high-resolution image.

For each patch in the high-resolution coarse image, we find the closest patch in the low-resolution coarse image. Then, the high-frequency band, or missing detail, for this patch can be assumed to be the patch at the same position in the low-resolution, high-frequency band. This simple idea, initially shown by Freeman, Jones, and Pasztor (2002) and Freedman and Fattal (2011), provides a powerful framework that can be used (with convenient modifications) even for video upscaling (Salvador, Kochale, & Schweidler, 2013). In general, it is also convenient to pay special attention to the design of the interpolation and analysis filters, because different patch contents (including different degrees of texture and structure) are better preserved by filters with different selectivity vs. ringing trade-offs (Salvador, Pérez-Pellitero, & Kochale, 2013). A different alternative to provide nonparametric adaptive filters within a detail transfer setup is shown in J. Yang et al. (2013). Additional considerations on the properties of image and noise signals also lead to robust methods, as in the joint upscaling and

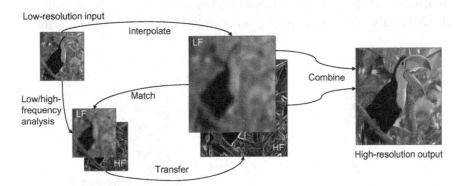

Fig. 2.1 *In the high-frequency transfer approach, a coarse version of the high-resolution image is initially obtained via interpolation. After conveniently analyzing the (full-spectrum) input image into a coarse or low-frequency band and a corresponding fine-detail, or high-frequency counterpart, the high-frequency is transferred for each patch in the high-resolution image to produce the super-resolved image.*

denoising method presented in Salvador et al. (2014). More details behind the design of high-frequency transfer methods are given in Chapter 3.

2.2.2 Neighbor Embedding

The general idea behind the neighbor embedding (or locally linear embedding) framework (Roweis & Saul, 2000) is that each input data vector (i.e., a low-resolution patch) can be described as a linear combination of its nearest neighbors on the natural image manifold of low-resolution patches. The application for super resolution is possible since this description is also valid across scales, assuming local geometric similarities of low and high-resolution spaces. As shown in Fig. 2.2, given the higher-dimensional patches corresponding to the nearest neighbors in low-resolution, the high-resolution version of the patch can consequently be obtained by the linear combination of the high-resolution neighbors with the same linear weights obtained in low-resolution.

This idea, which was originally presented by Freeman et al. (2002) and Chang, Yeung, and Xiong (2004) in scenarios with external examples from a training set, has been successfully adopted in the last years in internal learning. In Türkan, Thoreau, and Guillotel (2012), a method based on multiscale neighbor embeddings of image patches is presented, which, inspired by manifold learning approaches, first characterizes the local geometry of low-resolution patches by reconstructing them from similar patches taken from downscaled versions of the input image. The high-resolution patches are hallucinated by relying on the local geometric similarities of the low and high-resolution patch spaces. Bevilacqua et al. (2012) also considers, among other options, internal learning with a

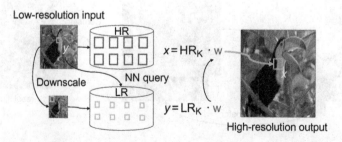

Fig. 2.2 In the neighbor embedding approach for internal learning, the input image is downscaled and large patches in the original image and small patches in the downscaled image are used to create a database of related high-resolution and low-resolution patches. Then, each small patch in the original image is described as a weighted combination of its nearest neighbors in the low-resolution database, and the large high-resolution patch is computed as the same weighted combination from the corresponding patches in the high-resolution database.

nonnegative variation of neighbor embedding and the use of gradient-based features for describing patches. The nonnegative neighbor embedding is based on the solution of a nonnegative least squares problem for each patch (Lawson & Hanson, 1974).

Several variations on the reconstruction pipeline for super resolution with internal learning have been presented in the last years. In Türkan, Thoreau, and Guillotel (2013), the size of each low-resolution patch is gradually expanded (1 pixel per iteration) by relying on local geometric similarities of low- and high-resolution patch spaces under small scaling factors. The local geometry is characterized with k-similar patches taken from the exemplar set, which is updated with collected exemplar patch pairs from the input image and its rescaled versions. An enhanced level of local compatibility is obtained with an optimization on k. In Türkan, Thoreau, and Guillotel (2014), sparsity-constrained neighbor embeddings is proposed, in an iterative fashion, to refine the high-resolution image. More recently, in Türkan, Alain, Thoreau, Guillotel, and Guillemot (2015) a more generic epitome learning scheme (Cheung, Frey, & Jojic, 2005; Jojic, Frey, & Kannan, 2003) with increased optimality, compactness, and reconstruction stability is presented for video upscaling applications. More details behind the design of neighbor embedding methods are given in Chapter 4.

2.3 EXTERNAL LEARNING

One of the computational limitations in internal learning methods exploiting cross-scale self-similarity is that the processing must be iteratively applied in small scaling factors to ensure the self-similarity assumption, which translates into a costly processing. Furthermore, as pointed out by Bevilacqua et al. (2012), the use of an external database of examples for neighbor embedding can actually outperform the internal learning approach in terms of generalization. The runtime of neighbor embedding with external examples can be reasonably improved by either:

- Approximate nearest-neighbor search methods based on hashing, for databases of extracted example patches (Heo et al., 2012; Korman & Avidan, 2011).
- Approximate nearest-neighbor field methods, for databases with entire images (Barnes et al., 2010; He & Sun, 2012; Torres et al., 2014).

However, a better trade-off in generalization vs. computational load (including both memory usage and runtime) can be reached by more efficient schemes.

For example, the kernel ridge regression (KRR) framework (K. I. Kim & Kwon, 2010) learns a map from input low-resolution images to target high-resolution ones based on example pairs of input and output images. A sparse solution, combining the ideas of kernel matching pursuit and gradient descent, allows reducing the time complexity for both training and testing. As a regularized solution, KRR leads to a better generalization than simply storing the examples, as in early example-based algorithms (Freeman et al., 2000) and results in much robuster reconstruction.

In the following, we discuss recent approaches for external learning: First, sparse coding approaches based on unsupervised learning; then anchored regression, including supervised learning during the training stage for more efficient inference. A further step in terms of inference efficiency, with an alternative unsupervised learning scheme, is provided by regression trees and forests. Finally, we include some notes on the existing approaches based on deep learning with convolutional networks (LeCun et al., 1989; Rumelhart, Hinton, & Williams, 1988).

2.3.1 Sparse Coding

Sparse coding-based regression techniques (Pérez-Pellitero, Salvador, Ruiz-Hidalgo, & Rosenhahn, 2013; J. Yang et al., 2010; Zeyde, Elad, & Protter, 2012) improve over neighbor embedding by providing a compact or sparse dictionary that can be obtained by unsupervised learning on either the low-resolution examples, for example, using the K-SVD algorithm (Aharon, Elad, & Bruckstein, 2006), or on both the low- and high-resolution pairs (J. Yang et al., 2010).

During the training stage in J. Yang et al. (2010), a large set of patches extracted from natural images and their downscaled (low-resolution) counterparts are used to generate two coupled sparse dictionaries, one for high-resolution D_h, and another one for low-resolution D_l.

The general idea of the inference stage in the basic sparse coding approaches (J. Yang et al., 2010; Zeyde et al., 2012), depicted in Fig. 2.3, is to decompose each low-resolution image patch y as a sparse linear combination of base patches, or atoms from the overcomplete low-resolution

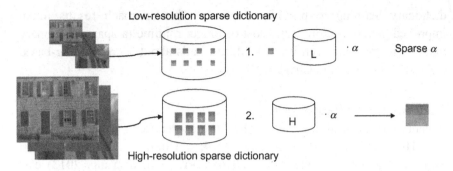

Fig. 2.3 In the sparse coding approach, an external, yet compact database formed by a low-resolution to high-resolution is obtained by offline training. During the inference stage, the input image is divided into patches; each patch is first described as a sparse linear combination of the atoms in the low-resolution dictionary, and the same coefficients are used with the atoms in the high-resolution dictionary to generate the high-resolution patch.

dictionary D_l. This results in a costly optimization process for each patch that can be expressed as

$$\min_{\alpha} \|y - D_l\alpha\|_2^2 + \lambda\|\alpha\|_0. \tag{2.2}$$

The data term enforces similarity between the observed patch and the reconstruction, whereas the sparse regularization term enforces a small number of nonzero entries in the decomposition α. The reconstruction of the high-resolution patch x is straight-forward, once α is known: $x = D_h\alpha$, and the full image reconstruction can be accomplished by overlapping all reconstructed patches.

Even though the dictionary size is drastically reduced with respect to neighbor embedding techniques, and so the search times, the execution time of the inference stage is still lengthy. Major improvements on both accuracy and speed are obtained by Zeyde et al. (2012) with the adoption of the K-SVD algorithm to train a coarse dictionary (from coarse patches only, without involving the high-resolution ones in the optimization) and Orthogonal Matching Pursuit (OMP) (Tropp & Gilbert, 2007) to solve the decomposition problem, similar to the one in Eq. (2.2), during the inference stage. Despite the improvements, the use of OMP during inference is still clearly the bottleneck of this approach.

Toward improved generalization, the Local Naive Bayes framework by McCann and Lowe (2012) is adopted by Pérez-Pellitero et al. (2013) to select semantically meaningful image regions, and combined with sparse dictionary learning to provide adaptivity. This approach results in an improved generalization at the cost of longer runtime (a sparse dictionary must be learned for each image). More details about sparse coding-based techniques are given in Chapter 5.

2.3.2 Anchored Regression

Recent external learning approaches (Pérez-Pellitero, Salvador, Torres, Ruiz-Hidalgo, & Rosenhahn, 2014; Timofte et al., 2013; Timofte, De Smet, & Van Gool, 2014; C.-Y. Yang & Yang, 2013) cast the super-resolution problem as a mapping from either low-resolution, or coarse (upscaled by interpolation), patches to high-resolution ones in a single step. Because the mapping function is nonlinear, it is beneficial to split it into locally linear mapping functions. During offline training, low-resolution or coarse patches can be clustered (e.g., extracting centroids with K-SVD) during an unsupervised stage. Under the assumption of linearity close to each centroid, the mapping function can then be approximated by a regression matrix by introducing supervised learning to the offline training. The advantage of these approaches is a streamlined inference (Fig. 2.4):

1. Determine the best cluster (linearization) for each patch
2. Apply the precomputed linear mapping function to each patch
3. Reconstruct the high-resolution image by patch overlapping

The Anchored Neighbor Regression (ANR) algorithm by Timofte et al. (2013) proposed to relax the sparsity constraint in Eq. (2.2) and anchor the set of most similar atoms to each entry, resulting in a L_2-regularized

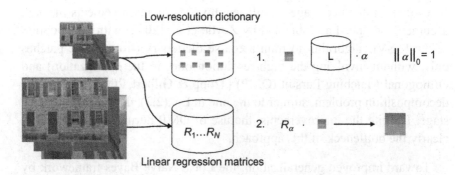

Fig. 2.4 *In the anchored regression approach, an external database composed of a low-resolution dictionary and a set of linear regression matrices to map the low-resolution examples to their high-resolution counterparts is computed offline. During the inference stage, the input image is divided into patches; each patch is matched to the nearest atom in the low-resolution dictionary and the corresponding regression matrix is used to generate the high-resolution patch.*

regression problem that can be computed in closed form during training, instead to having to find a costly iterative solution to the former L_0-regularized problem:

$$\min_{\alpha} \|y - N_l(y)\alpha\|_2^2 + \lambda \|\alpha\|_2^2, \qquad (2.3)$$

where $N_l(y)$ contains just the nearest neighbors within D_l of one of the atoms. The resulting linear mapping for the chosen atom in the dictionary is $N_h(y)\alpha$, where $N_h(y)$ is the high-resolution counterpart to $N_l(y)$.

The Simple Functions approach by C.-Y. Yang and Yang (2013) proposes an alternative model, where clustering is applied directly onto low-resolution patches and then a separate mapping from low-resolution to high-resolution patches is learned. Their simple mapping function of choice is an affine transformation that can be learned offline for each cluster. Again, a practical limitation of the method is that the affine mapping for each patch is determined by an exhaustive search over all possible clusters during the inference stage.

More recently, Pérez-Pellitero et al. (2014) and Timofte et al. (2014) have proposed obtaining a dictionary trained with K-SVD like Timofte et al. (2013) with the difference that, instead of learning the linear regression function of each atom in the dictionary using only other atoms, the entire set of training samples are used. This produces a better sampling of the coarse manifold and also provides a unification of C.-Y. Yang and Yang (2013) and Timofte et al. (2013). More details about anchored regression techniques are given in Chapter 6.

2.3.3 Regression Trees

As hinted above, perhaps the most affecting practical bottleneck in anchored regression is the exhaustive search stage (Timofte et al., 2013, 2014; C.-Y. Yang & Yang, 2013). One possible solution is presented in Pérez-Pellitero et al. (2014), where a fast nearest-neighbor search is built such that the clustering induced by the K-SVD dictionary atoms can be efficiently exploited in the inference stage, resulting in large speed-ups. The idea is to construct this fast search strategy based on Spherical Hashing (Heo et al., 2012) to get logarithmic-time access to the anchor points obtained by K-SVD (and their corresponding linear mapping functions). A less efficient solution to this scalability problem is the hierarchical search scheme by Timofte, Rothe, and Van Gool (2016).

An alternative, and more uniform, solution is to perform unsupervised hierarchical clustering, e.g., Freund, Dasgupta, Kabra, and Verma (2007) and McNames (2001), to learn the patch subspace. This strategy allows determining clusters of similar patches (or features thereof) without the need for an additional dictionary learning method, and also to provide an intrinsic logarithmic-time search during the inference stage. One of the first applications of regression trees for super resolution appeared in the iterative in-place regression method by J. Yang et al. (2013), using the random projections approach by Freund et al. (2007). A slower, but better performing alternative is the PCA tree for subspace learning by McNames (2001), which requires computing the PCA of the elements in each hierarchical cluster during the offline training stage.

The general idea behind the application of regression trees in a single upscaling step is illustrated in Fig. 2.5. The pipeline is very similar to that in anchored regression, but has the advantage of a logarithmic search for the local regression function, versus the linear cost in the former. In the partition tree in the illustration, we start from the root (top) node and, based on a projection test, we proceed down the tree going to the left or the right child of each node until reaching a leaf node, which contains a regression matrix. The logarithmic search induced by the hierarchical clustering strategy has clear advantages with denser or finer samplings of the patch subspace, that is, with several thousands of local linearizations.

More recently, Schulter, Leistner, and Bischof (2015) and J. B. Huang et al. (2015) have also proposed to combine regressions from ensembles of random trees (Breiman, 2001; Criminisi, Shotton, & Konukoglu, 2011)

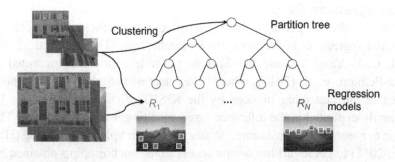

Fig. 2.5 *Regression trees provide a partition of the low-resolution space and a regression model for each subspace (leaf node). During the inference stage, the input image is divided into patches; each patch traverses the tree from the root (top node) to the most suitable leaf, and the corresponding regression model is used to generate the high-resolution patch.*

to improve accuracy and generalization for super resolution with a single iteration. Hierarchical approaches with a single regression tree solve the problem of subspace learning or clustering and provide efficient inference, but tree ensembles may still be too costly for real-time algorithms in most platforms. The reason behind this cost is due to the matrix-vector multiplication that produces the output patch. With a single tree, this operation is relatively inexpensive, but when regression matrices need to be fetched and applied for a large number of trees, the computational cost can become prohibitive for real-time applications. A solution to this problem is presented by Salvador and Pérez-Pellitero (2015), where, during traversal, the most suitable tree(s) can be chosen such that the regression quality is comparable to that of using all trees in the ensemble, but with the advantage of a dramatically reduced computational cost. More details about regression trees and forests applied to super resolution are given in Chapter 7.

2.3.4 Deep Learning

Last, but not least, the book also reviews the current alternatives with supervised learning approaches based on deep convolutional neural networks (LeCun et al., 1989). The main idea behind these techniques is to exploit the power of the back-propagation algorithm (Rumelhart et al., 1988) in order to learn hierarchical representations that allow for minimizing the error at the end of the network.

The adoption of convolutional networks is pervasive in image processing and computer vision applications, because they allow efficiently exploiting:

- **Stationarity**. The same response to a feature in the image (texture, color, edge) is expected independently of translations.
- **Locality**. The response to a feature is caused by local measurements around the feature.

Even relatively shallow convolutional networks provide performance similar to state-of-the-art anchored or forest-based regression models. Fig. 2.6 illustrates an arbitrarily deep network simply composed of the concatenation of convolutional and nonlinear layers. In this type of network, where the size and number of channels (or filters) in each convolutional layer has to be predefined, the training stage obtains the set of coefficients or parameters for each of the filters in each of the layers. For the nonlinear layers, it is a

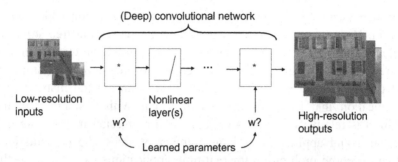

Fig. 2.6 *The convolutional networks framework allow learning the end-to-end mapping from low-resolution images to high-resolution ones by means of the cascaded application of convolutional and nonlinear layers. The coefficients of the convolutional layers can be learned during an offline stage with a large exemplars dataset.*

common practice to employ rectifying linear units, which greatly simplify the training stage for deep networks (Nair & Hinton, 2010).

The most intuitive application of convolutional neural networks for super resolution is the one in Dong, Loy, He, and Tang (2014, 2016). Similar to the structure in Fig. 2.6, the network is composed of two nonlinear layers in-between three convolutional layers, with the difference that the network doe not need to upconvert the image sizes. For that purpose, the low-resolution inputs are first upscaled using an interpolation method, and the resulting coarse approximations of the high-resolution images are then used to estimate the final high-resolution output.

A more promising venue for future research, is the introduction of domain-knowledge in more sophisticated architectures like the one proposed by Z. Wang, Liu, Yang, Han, and Huang (2015). The design of the network is driven by the combination of conventional sparse coding models and deep learning to achieve further improved results thanks to the fine-tuning ability of the back-propagation algorithm. Sparse coding can be embedded in deep networks by means of the cascaded approximation to the iterative shrinkage-thresholding algorithm (Gregor & LeCun, 2010). More details behind the design and training of deep networks can be found in Chapter 8.

2.4 DISCUSSION

In this chapter we have reviewed the different algorithmic approaches for example-based super-resolution, first understanding the differences between

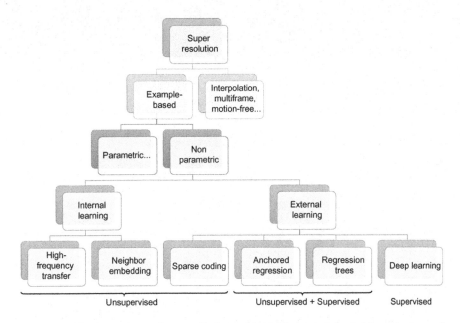

Fig. 2.7 The machine learning approaches covered by the rest of the book (bottom, including both internal and external-learning alternatives) in the context of the super-resolution taxonomy.

parametric and nonparametric methods. The powerful properties of machine learning-based nonparametric methods can, in turn, be classified into two types of methods (internal and external learning), based on the source of examples. The hierarchy of the machine learning techniques reviewed in this chapter and covered by the book is shown in Fig. 2.7. In the rest of the book, we focus on the two families of nonparametric methods, starting with two chapters on the internal learning methods based on high-frequency transfer and neighbor embedding. The next group of four chapters covers the most successful approaches for external learning, namely sparse coding, anchored regression, regression trees and forests, and deep learning.

CHAPTER 3

High-Frequency Transfer

We have already seen that when using interpolation-based upscaling methods (e.g., bicubic or bilinear), the resulting high-resolution image presents a frequency spectrum with shrunk support. Interpolation cannot fill in the missing high-frequency band up to the wider Nyquist limit for the upscaled image. High-frequency transfer allows for estimating the high-frequency band by combining high-frequency examples extracted from the input image and added to the interpolated low-frequency band, based on mechanisms akin to the one used by Freedman and Fattal (2011).

As shown by Glasner et al. (2009), natural images present the cross-scale self-similarity property. This basically results in a high probability of finding very similar small patches across different scales of the same image. Let

$$X_l = H_s * (Y \uparrow s) \tag{3.1}$$

be an upscaled version of the input image Y, with H_s a linear interpolation kernel, and s the upscaling factor. The subscript l refers to the fact that this upscaled image only contains the low-frequency band of the spectrum (with normalized bandwidth $1/s$). In general, we can assume that H_s has a low-pass behavior.

In this chapter we visit three methods to provide robust high-frequency transfer based on internal learning. In the first place, we discuss how to select suitable image filters in order to provide high-quality reconstruction of structure (or edges) and texture. Then, we proceed to considerations about neutralizing the localized presence of aliasing in the input image, and finally we cover the case of noisy input images.

3.1 ADAPTIVE FILTER SELECTION

The input image Y can be analyzed into two separate bands by using the same interpolation kernel employed for upscaling. Thus, we can compute

$$Y_l = H_s * Y \quad \text{and} \quad Y_h = Y - Y_l, \tag{3.2}$$

respectively, the low-frequency and high-frequency bands. By doing so, we are generating pairs of low-frequency references (in Y_l) and their

Example-Based Super Resolution. http://dx.doi.org/10.1016/B978-0-12-809703-8.00003-4

corresponding high-frequency examples (in Y_h). We should note that Y_l has the same normalized bandwidth as X_l and, most importantly, that the cross-scale self-similarity property is also present between these two images.

Let $x_{l,i}$ be a patch of $N_p \times N_p$ pixels with the central pixel located at $\lambda(x_{l,i}) = (r_i, c_i)$ within X_l. We look for the best matching patch in the low-resolution low-frequency band $y_{l,j} = \arg\min_{y_{l,j}} \|y_{l,j} - x_{l,i}\|_1$. Abusing notation, $\|x\|_P$ is the P-norm of the vectorized patch x. The location of $y_{l,j}$ is $\lambda(y_{l,j})$, and this is also the location of the corresponding high-frequency example $y_{h,j}$. The search can be constrained to a very localized window of size $N_w \times N_w$ pixels around $\lambda(x_{l,i})/s$, assuming that it is more likely to find a suitable example in a location close to the original, than further away (Freedman & Fattal, 2011; J. Yang et al., 2013).

The local estimate of the high-frequency band corresponding to a patch $x_{l,i}$ can be directly regressed as $x_{h,i} = y_{h,j}$. However, in order to ensure continuity and also to reduce the contribution of inconsistent high-frequency examples, the patch selection is done with a sliding window (or overlapping patches), which means that up to $N_p \times N_p$ high-frequency estimates are available for each pixel location. We can find the estimate for the high-frequency pixel as the average of the contributions, although different methods might slightly improve the reconstruction.

Once the above procedure is applied for each pixel in the upscaled image, the resulting high-frequency band X_h might still contain low-frequency spectral components because (1) filters are not ideal and (2) the operations leading to X_h do not correspond to a linear space-invariant system. Thus, in order to improve the spectral compatibility between X_l and X_h, we can subtract the low-frequency spectral component from X_h before adding it to the low-frequency band to compose the reconstructed image

$$\hat{X} = X_l + X_h - H_s * X_h. \tag{3.3}$$

3.1.1 Parametric Filter Design

In Fig. 3.1A and B we show how the method described above behaves when considering different designs for the interpolation kernel (or low-pass filters) H_s. Overall, the choice of a selective filter provides a good texture reconstruction in the super-resolved image, whereas filters with small selectivity tend to miss texture details with the advantage of avoiding ringing. This variability results from the nonstationary nature of image

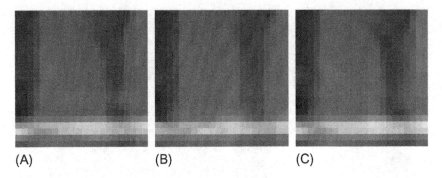

(A)   (B)   (C)

Fig. 3.1 Effects of filter H_S selection (2× upscaling). (A) A very selective filter provides detailed texture in the super-resolved image, but also produces ringing. (B) A filter with small selectivity reduces ringing, but fails to reconstruct texture. (C) Texture is reconstructed with reduced ringing by locally selecting a suitable filter.

statistics, and encourages us to locally select the most suitable filter type for each region in the image. In Fig. 3.1C we show how this strategy allows for reconstructing texture in areas with small contrast, while avoiding ringing in regions with higher contrast (e.g., around edges).

We can, for example, choose the well-known raised cosine filter (Y. Lin, Chen, Jiang, & Hsai, 2004) to provide a range of parametric kernels with different levels of selectivity. The analytic expression of a one-dimensional raised cosine filter is

$$H_{s,\beta}(t) = \frac{\sin(\pi st)}{\pi st} \frac{\cos(\pi s\beta t)}{1 - 4s^2\beta^2 t^2}, \tag{3.4}$$

where s is the upscaling factor (the normalized bandwidth of the filter is $1/s$) and β is the roll-off factor (which measures the excess bandwidth of the filter). Since all the upscaling and low-pass filtering operations are separable, this expression is applied for both the vertical and horizontal axis, consecutively. We enforce the value of β to lie in the range $[0, s-1]$, so that the excess bandwidth never exceeds the Nyquist frequency. With $\beta = 0$ we obtain the most selective filter (with a large amount of ringing) and, with $\beta = s-1$, the least selective one.

In order to adaptively select the most suitable filter from a bank of $N_f = 5$ filters with $\beta = \{0, \frac{s-1}{4}, \frac{s-1}{2}, 3\frac{s-1}{4}, s-1\}$, we can look for the one providing minimal matching cost for each overlapping patch, as described in the following. Fig. 3.2 shows the shade-encoded chosen filter (ranging from the darkest shade for $\beta = 0$, to the lightest one, for $\beta = s-1$) for each patch. We denote by $x_{\beta,l,i}$, $x_{\beta,h,i}$, $y_{\beta,l,j}$, and $y_{\beta,h,j}$ a low-frequency patch, the

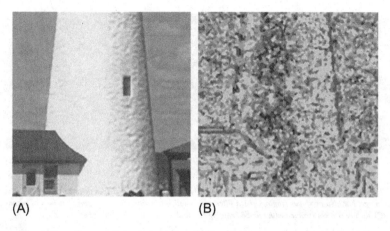

(A)   (B)

Fig. 3.2 Adaptive filter selection. (A) detail of a super-resolved image (2× magnification). (B) selected filters from a set of five raised cosine filters with β = {0, 1/4, 1/2, 3/4, 1}. Note how the statistical distribution of the selected filter reflects the nonstationary statistics of the image.

corresponding reconstructed high-frequency patch, the best matching low-resolution reference patch, and the corresponding high-frequency example patch, respectively, which have been obtained by using the interpolation kernel and analysis filter $H_{s,\beta}$. Then, we can measure the local kernel cost as

$$k_{\beta,i} = \alpha \|x_{\beta,l,i} - y_{\beta,l,j}\|_1 + (1 - \alpha)\|x_{\beta,h,i} - y_{\beta,h,j}\|_1. \qquad (3.5)$$

The parameter α tunes the filter selection. As shown in Fig. 3.3, small values of α (ignoring low-frequency differences) tend to a more uniform selection of filters, whereas large values of α (ignoring high-frequency differences) typically result in the selection of ringing-free filters, with worse separation of low and high-frequency bands. In general, large values of α tend to better qualitative and quantitative (PSNR, SSIM) results. The final

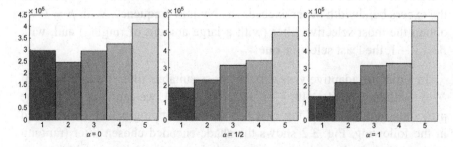

Fig. 3.3 Histogram of selected filters (for 2× magnification) from a set of five raised cosine filters with β = {0, 1/4, 1/2, 3/4, 1} for different values of the tuning parameter α. The shade mapping is the same of Fig. 3.2B.

high-resolution image is obtained by averaging the overlapping patches of the images computed with the selected filters.

Implementation Notes

The costlier sections (example search, composition stages, filtering) can be easily parallelized in OpenMP, OpenCL, or CUDA. A reasonable choice for the patch side is $N_p = 3$ pixels and the search window side can be set to $N_w = 15$ or smaller for shorter runtime. The algorithm must be applied iteratively with small upscaling steps ($s = s_1 s_2 \ldots$), for example, an upscaling with $s = 2$ can be implemented as an initial upscaling with $s_1 = 4/3$ and a second one with $s_2 = 3/2$. Apart from considerations about the higher degree of self-similarity for small magnification factors, the wider available bandwidth for matching also results in a better selection of high-frequency examples at the cost of an increased computational cost.

As a postprocessing stage, we can apply Iterative Back-Projection (Irani & Peleg, 1991; J. Yang et al., 2010) to ensure that the information of the input image is completely contained in the high-resolution estimate:

$$X^{(n+1)} := X^{(n)} + H_u * ((Y - (X^{(n)} * H_d) \downarrow s) \uparrow s). \qquad (3.6)$$

The algorithm typically converges after two or three iterations. The upscaling (H_u) and downscaling (H_d) kernels are the ones corresponding bicubic resizing.

3.1.2 Performance

Commonly used datasets in example-based super-resolution include *Kodak*, with 24 images of 768×512 pixels, or the 500 images in the *Berkeley* segmentation dataset from the project website of Arbelaez, Maire, Fowlkes, and Malik (2011), with 481×321 pixels each. To quantitatively assess the performance of the filter selection method, we choose a subset of 20 images from *Berkeley* and all 24 images from *Kodak*.

Apart from comparing to the bicubic interpolation baseline, we also choose two example-based methods: The sparse coding approach by J. Yang et al. (2010), which we refer to by *sparse*; and kernel ridge regression by K. I. Kim and Kwon (2010), which we refer to by *ridge*. The latter includes a postprocessing stage based on the natural image prior (Tappen, Russell, & Freeman, 2003). For *sparse*, we use the dictionary obtained with the default training dataset and standard parameters.

The comparison consists of downscaling each image by a factor of $1/s$ using bicubic resizing and upscaling the low-resolution version by a factor of s with each method. For $s = 2$, we include the Structural Similarity (SSIM) and Y-PSNR (Peak Signal to Noise Ratio measured on the luminance channel) quantitative metrics and the runtime in Fig. 3.4. As expected, we observe that all super-resolution methods perform better than the baseline bicubic interpolation, with *ridge* and the filter selection method also improving over *sparse*. This reflects the good generalization of the internal learning strategy in comparison to early sparse coding. In terms of runtime, the high-frequency transfer is clearly faster than the other tested super-resolution methods thanks to the small search windows. Fig. 3.5 shows sample results obtained with both datasets.

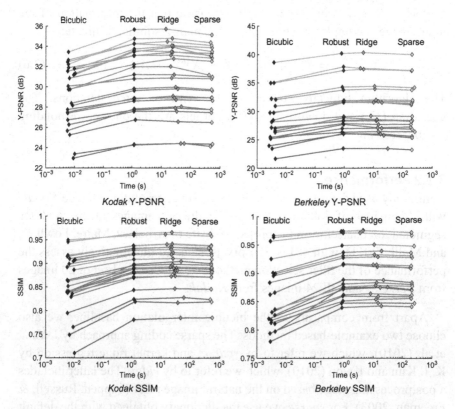

Fig. 3.4 Top, Y-PSNR vs. time for the Kodak (left) and Berkeley (right) datasets. Bottom, SSIM vs. time. The multifilter high-frequency transfer method (proposed) is competitive in both speed and accuracy.

Fig. 3.5 Sample results from the Kodak dataset for 2× upscaling, including the groundtruth image (top left), the reconstructed one with the filter selection method (top right), ridge (K. I. Kim & Kwon, 2010) (bottom left), and sparse (J. Yang et al., 2010) (bottom right).

3.2 ROBUSTNESS TO ALIASING

This section describes a mechanism to introduce robustness against artifacts due to the presence of aliasing in the input image. In contrast to the previous section, and for the sake of clarity, here we consider a simpler scenario where only one filter is available, but a similar principle can be combined with the filter selection strategy described above.

3.2.1 Local Regularization

The block diagram of the system with robustness to aliasing is shown in Fig. 3.6. Y refers to the input low-resolution image, Y_l and Y_h correspond to the low-frequency (LF) and high-frequency (HF) bands of the low-resolution frame, X_l and X_h are the high-resolution counterparts, and X is the resulting high-resolution image. In the following, we detail the

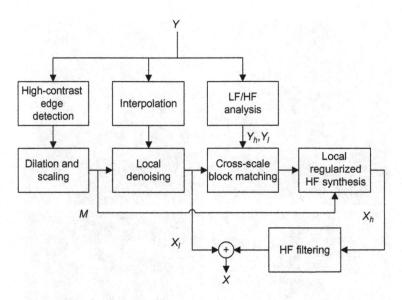

Fig. 3.6 Block diagram of a high-frequency transfer system robust to aliasing.

contribution of the new blocks, that is, high-contrast edge detection, dilation and scaling; local denoising; and locally regularized HF synthesis.

High-Contrast Edge Detection, Dilation and Scaling
A binary mask M is obtained as the summed response of a classical pair of vertical and horizontal *Sobel* filters, which can then be thresholded and thinned previous to a morphologic dilation stage (with a compact structuring element, for example, of size 3) and posterior nearest-neighbor resizing to the target output resolution (the resulting mask has values $M = 1$ in regions where aliasing is likely to appear and $M = 0$ elsewhere).

Local Denoising
Then, the pixels of the low-frequency band obtained by interpolation (e.g., using bicubic or raised cosine kernels) for $M = 1$ can be estimated by imposing Total Variation regularization, which cancels out small fluctuations (typical manifestation of aliasing), while preserving structure (edges). This last process can be interpreted as a local denoising and quickly solved with an iterative algorithm.

Locally Regularized HF Synthesis
The synthesized high-frequency band of the high-resolution image X_h is set to the average of the overlapping contributions of the high-frequency

Fig. 3.7 From left to right, detail of 4× super resolution using Glasner et al. (2009) and Freedman and Fattal (2011), and high-frequency transfer with local denoising.

example patches. Then total variation is again applied for those pixels where $M = 1$ to avoid undesired variations due to aliasing.

3.2.2 Performance

Fig. 3.7 shows a detailed view of results obtained with different techniques for 4× upscaling. Compared to the high-frequency transfer method by Freedman and Fattal (2011), the incorporation of local denoising shows less false contours (e.g., shape of letter A) and, compared to the multiscale approach by Glasner et al. (2009), a reduced amount of artifacts derived from the presence of aliasing (e.g., in transversal direction to the long edge).

Fig. 3.8 shows some examples of the advantage of using local denoising when the input image shows obvious aliasing artifacts around high-contrast contours.

3.3 ROBUSTNESS TO NOISE

High-frequency transfer can also be modified to incorporate awareness and correction for images corrupted with additive noise. One possible approach consists of adapting the in-place cross-scale self-similarity prior (Zontak et al., 2013) to the super-resolution problem. An overview of the resulting approach is shown in Fig. 3.9. The main idea is to exploit the cleaner appearance of patches in downscaled versions of the input image to learn robuster fine-detail examples.

Fig. 3.8 *Top left, detail of an input image with aliasing artifacts around high-contrast edges (jaggies); top right, upscaling (2×) using bicubic interpolation; bottom left, using high-frequency transfer without local denoising; bottom right, using local denoising. Note the reduced amount of oscillations around edges affected by aliasing (when compared to the method without local denoising), and the enhanced resolution (when compared to bicubic interpolation).*

Let X be a noiseless high-resolution image and Y the noisy downscaled observation, that is,

$$Y = (X * H_s)\downarrow(s,s) + N, \tag{3.7}$$

where H_s is a suitable (antialiasing) interpolation filter, $\downarrow(s,s)$ is a downscaling operator producing an image s times smaller than the original one along each spatial axis and N is white additive noise.

It is well known that natural images often show a decaying spectrum, that is, $S_x(\Omega) \sim 1/\Omega^2$, where $S_x(\Omega)$ is the power spectral density of the clean image X and Ω is a norm of the 2D normalized spatial frequency, that is, $\Omega = ||\Omega||_a$, with $\Omega = (\Omega_1, \Omega_2)$ for some $0 < a \leq 2$. If we now consider the frequency-domain SNR behavior of the degraded image Y, i.e., $\text{SNR}_y(\Omega)$,

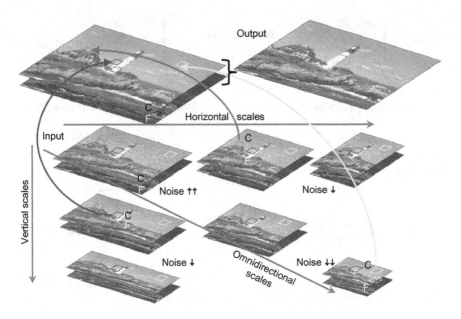

Fig. 3.9 Overview of an approach for high-frequency transfer with robustness to noise. The roof (tower, sky) patch, dominated by a horizontal (vertical, omnidirectional) structure, is reconstructed from the optimal scale in the horizontal (vertical, omnidirectional) multiscale pyramid, thus trading off noise level and structure similarity. The reconstruction strategy allows for simultaneously reducing noise in the coarse (C) interpolated band, and adding fine (F) detail learned from lower-resolution scales.

we can observe that it also decays quadratically with Ω given the flat shape of $S_n(\Omega)$ (white noise).

Interpolation-based super resolution (e.g., bicubic) generates a coarse estimate of X as

$$X_c = [Y\!\uparrow\!(s,s)] * H_u, \tag{3.8}$$

such that $S_{x_c}(\Omega) \cong S_y(s\Omega) \mid 0 \leq \Omega < \Omega_c = 1/2s$. The main task of a high-frequency transfer algorithm is to fill in the higher band of the spectrum ($\Omega_c \leq \Omega < 1/2$), which can be accomplished by exploiting strong statistics in natural images, that is, cross-scale self-similarity.

As intuitively shown in Fig. 3.10, the fine-detail band obtained by SI-SR is directly estimated from the fine-detail band of the input image, which is also the noisiest due to the quadratically decreasing behavior of the frequency-domain SNR. Therefore, the noisiest part of the spectrum receives a higher weight (than in interpolation-based upscaling), resulting in a degraded average SNR. Our goal is, thus, to estimate the extended

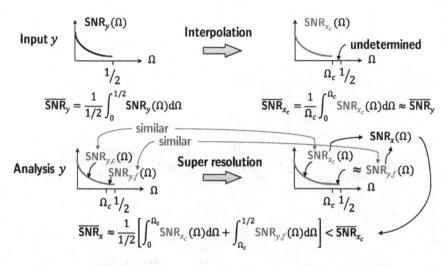

Fig. 3.10 *SNR degradation after super resolution via internal learning. Note how the noisiest part of the frequency-domain of the SNR (the fine detail beyond Ω_c) influences a larger part of the spectrum after applying super resolution. This extended support results in a higher weight, which in turn decreases the average SNR.*

spectrum by learning from examples with enhanced SNR, aiming at the minimization of this degradation.

3.3.1 In-Place Cross-Scale Self-Similarity

Cross-scale self-similarity, introduced by Glasner et al. (2009), has been a widely utilized prior for internal learning super-resolution algorithms. Its main advantage is the adaptivity to the image contents. Whereas this type of prior was originally presented while considering all possible locations within all possible scales as references, posterior results—such as those provided by Freedman and Fattal (2011), where the search range for examples is restricted to a small rectangular window in a single scale, or J. Yang et al. (2013), where conditions are determined for further reducing the search space to a single location (*in-place* example) when combined with linear regression—have progressively allowed improvement in the efficiency of SR approaches without losing accuracy. An often omitted question is the extension of these powerful priors to the case of noisy images. This problem has been recently addressed by Zontak et al. (2013) in a denoising scenario.

In-place Structure Similarity

Let $Y_{U,V}$ denote an image obtained by downscaling by $s_U = \alpha^U$ and $s_V = \alpha^V$ (where $\alpha < 1$ is an analysis downscaling factor) along each major axis, that is, $Y_{U,V} = (Y*H_{U,V})\downarrow(s_U, s_V)$. Let $y_{0,0} \in Y_{0,0} \equiv Y$ be a small patch of $p \times p$ pixels (of image data or other features) with its center located in some normalized coordinates (i.e., coordinates such that $(0,0)$ and $(1,1)$ refer to the top left and bottom right corners of the image, respectively). It is very likely to find a patch $y_{U,V} \in Y_{U,V}$ at exactly the same normalized coordinates, and such that $y_{U,V} \approx y_{0,0}$ for some scale indices $U, V \geq 0$. Note that subscripts refer to scales; the optimal one can then be determined as

$$\hat{U}, \hat{V} = \underset{U,V}{\arg\min} \|y_{0,0} - y_{U,V}\|_2^2, \tag{3.9}$$

which will most likely result in scales close to the original (indices $U = 0, V = 0$) when Y is not corrupted by noise, because structure similarity is naturally stronger when images (or other features) are of similar scales.

Noisy In-place Self-Similarity
Even if the input image contains a high level of noise, a downscaled version can be close to noiseless. Indeed, the image noise level σ, which exponentially decays when downscaling, can be approximated as

$$\sigma_{U,V} = \sigma_{0,0}\alpha^{U/2}\alpha^{V/2}, \tag{3.10}$$

where $\sigma_{0,0}$ is the noise level of the original image. An empirical confirmation is shown in Fig. 3.11. However, in-place structure similarity drops as scales become further apart. Thus, when looking for similar reference patches we

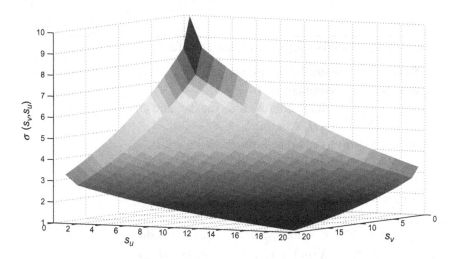

Fig. 3.11 The standard deviation of Gaussian white noise decays exponentially with the vertical and horizontal downscaling factors. The application of an antialiasing interpolation filter produces a larger gap around downscaling factors close to 1.

must trade-off structure similarity and noise level. Three examples of this situation are illustrated in Fig. 3.9, including patches with strong vertical (roof) and horizontal (tower) gradients and also an unstructured patch (sky). The optimal scale in the noisy case can be determined as

$$\hat{U}, \hat{V} = \arg\min_{U,V} \left\{ \|y_{0,0} - y_{U,V}\|_2^2 + 2\rho_{U,V}(\sigma_{0,0}) \right\}, \tag{3.11}$$

where $\rho_{U,V}(\sigma) = p^2\sigma^2\alpha^{U+V}$ is the approximate noise correlation between the $p{\times}p$ patch in the original scale and the in-place one in a scale with indices U, V.

3.3.2 Iterative Noise-Aware Super Resolution

The last remaining question is how to adapt this noise-aware prior to a frequency-transfer-based super-resolution application. The resulting method, which provides a joint denoising and high-quality upscaling of sharp, yet noisy input images, is summarized in Algorithm 1. It can be divided into four steps: (1) *interpolation*-based coarse upscaling; (2) coarse/fine *analysis* with multiscale pyramids; (3) *learning* of coarse/fine in-place examples from the most suitable scales (noise vs. structure trade-off); and (4) *reconstruction* by accumulation of the denoised learned contributions.

Algorithm 1 Robust High-Frequency Transfer

Data: Noisy image Y and upscaling factor s
Result: Upscaled image $\hat{X}$
$\sigma \leftarrow$ NoiseLevel(Y), from X. Liu, Tanaka, and Okutomi (2012)
$X_c \leftarrow [Y\!\uparrow(s,s)]*H_s$ (coarse), $\hat{X} \leftarrow \mathbf{0}$, $A \leftarrow \mathbf{0}$
for *each analysis scale U, V* **do**
   | $Y_{U,V} \leftarrow (Y*H_{U,V})\!\downarrow(s_U, s_V)$ (denoised)
   | $C_{U,V} \leftarrow Y_{U,V}*H_s$ (denoised coarse)
for *each patch $x_c \in X_c$ with $p_x = supp(x_c)$* **do**
   | $\epsilon \leftarrow \min_{U,V}\left\{\|x_c - c_{U,V}\|_2^2 + 2\rho_{U,V}(\sigma)\right\}$
   | **for** $U, V \mid \|x_c - c_{U,V}\|_2^2 + 2\rho_{U,V}(\sigma) < k{\cdot}\epsilon$ **do**
      | $\hat{X}(p_x) \leftarrow \hat{X}(p_x) + y_{U,V}$, $A(p_x) \leftarrow A(p_x) + 1$

return $\hat{X} \leftarrow \hat{X}/A$ (element-wise division)

Interpolation

In the first place, Y can be upscaled by a magnifying factor s using an interpolation-based approach. Despite the relevance of the choice of the optimal interpolation filter H_s has already been shown, here we can just use a single instance of a bicubic interpolation filter. The resulting X_c is a coarse (and noisy) estimate of the desired image X. Besides, the noise level σ of the input image Y is determined by using, for example, the method by X. Liu et al. (2012).

Analysis

A total number of $3 \times N_s - 2$ downscaled versions $Y_{U,V}$ of the input image are generated (similarly to the example shown in Fig. 3.9), where N_s is the number of scales along each of the three pyramids (horizontal, vertical, and omnidirectional or isotropic). The possible combinations of U, V are restricted to the scales $\{0, l\} \cup \{l, 0\} \cup \{l, l\}$ with $l = \{0, \dots, N_s\}$, that is, horizontal and vertical edge-preserving pyramids and an isotropic pyramid, respectively.

We also compute a coarse version of each scale by applying H_s, the same filter used for upscaling. Whereas each coarse $C_{U,V}$ provides estimates of (almost) noiseless versions of the coarse patches in X_c, the difference between the scaled image $Y_{U,V}$ and its corresponding $C_{U,V}$ is fine detail information, which is missing in X_c. As a result of this analysis, cross-scale self-similarity (and denoising) can be performed between the coarse versions (X_c and $\{C_{U,V}\}$) and joint denoising and super-resolution can be obtained from the richer information in $\{Y_{U,V}\}$.

Learning

We can use the known noise level and the analysis pyramids to determine the patch in a lower scale that best describes the structure of each coarse patch $x_c \in X_c$. The scale of the (coarse) in-place matching patch can be determined following the robust in-place self-similarity strategy in Eq. (3.11), with x_c and $c_{U,V}$ ($\in C_{U,V}$) replacing $y_{0,0}$ and $y_{U,V}$, respectively. The best matching patch and the next most similar ones (in scales showing a similarity cost up to k times that of the best one) should be considered possible realizations of the (coarse) latent noiseless patch, considering the variance on the noise process. By doing so, true optimal matches are included with higher probability than by just taking the best match. Fig. 3.12 shows the distribution of the most similar scales for all patches of an image corrupted with different noise levels. Because $\{Y_{U,V}\}$ can be interpreted as

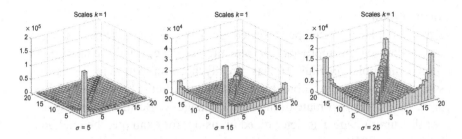

Fig. 3.12 *Distribution of the scale U, V of the noise-aware most similar patches of an image corrupted with different levels of noise σ. Note the selection of coarser scales with progressively noisier input.*

enriched (containing fine detail information) versions of the chosen $\{C_{U,V}\}$, super-resolution can be achieved by using the patches of the former.

Reconstruction
The final reconstruction stage is a simple averaging of the contributions of the example patches learned in the previous stage. Different weighting schemes might provide slight improvements in terms of the noise reduction vs. feature preservation trade-off.

Implementation Details
It is advisable to reach the desired magnification factor s iteratively (in smaller steps); for example, an upscaling with $s = 2$ can be implemented as an initial upscaling with $s_1 = 4/3$ and a second one with $s_2 = 3/2$. The wider available bandwidth for matching with smaller magnification factors results in a better selection of examples during learning. The first iterations should assume a noiseless scenario to keep as much information from the underlying noiseless image as possible throughout the upscaling stages. Thus, during these first iterations only the fine detail of the (single) best match is used to complement the interpolated coarse estimate. The last iteration uses the complete method in Algorithm 1, where the coarse band is both denoised and complemented with fine detail.

Further denoising performance is possible when combining the procedure above with the nonlocal means (NLM) algorithm from Buades, Coll, and Morel (2005) applied onto the $Y_{U,V}$ layers. By doing so, we can remove residual noise in the different levels of the pyramid. The noise for each scale is set from Eq. (3.10) and the search window radius is set to 1 pixel. The improvement lies in the order of 0.1 to 0.2 dB of Peak Signal to Noise Ratio (PSNR).

The optimal size of the patches is strongly related to the noise level. We can use fully overlapping patches (sliding window) of size defined by the noise level ($p = \{3, 5, 7\}$ for $\sigma < \{10, 20, \infty\}$, respectively) for a good and generalizable performance. The described method can be applied directly onto the luminance channel. For the chrominance channels, a simpler pipeline can be adopted with similar perceptual results, consisting of initial denoising (e.g., using the same cross-scale self-similarity prior) and interpolation to the desired scale. A reasonable dimensioning of the example pyramid is $N_s = 20$ analysis scales per pyramid, with an analysis downscaling factor $\alpha = 0.9$, but finer pyramids will, in general, provide better results at the expense of a higher computational cost.

3.3.3 Performance

We can test the approach by means of an objective evaluation, for example, on the 24 images of the Kodak dataset, and a subjective validation. The 24 images, which are used as groundtruth, are downscaled by a factor of $s = 2$ using bicubic interpolation and corrupted with 12 different levels ($\sigma = 0, 5, \ldots, 55$) of additive white Gaussian noise to build the input.

We include a number of recent, well-performing methods which do not include robustness in their formulation, including two anchored regression approaches by Timofte et al. (2013) (*Global Regression*, GR, and the adaptive *Anchored Neighborhood Regression*, ANR), the kernel regression approach with postprocessing based on the natural image prior by K. I. Kim and Kwon (2010) and the well-known sparse-dictionary approach by J. Yang et al. (2010), which is also postprocessed (with iterative back-projection). For the results from GR, ANR, and the robust high-frequency transfer method no postprocessing is applied, but we note that doing so greatly improves performance for the latter with low noise.

Visual inspection of the sample results in Fig. 3.13 subjectively validate the proposed approach. We can observe how this robust nonparametric prior is competent for super resolution with noticeable input noise levels (note the sharp edges with a relatively high noise level $\sigma = 15$, third row), whereas all other tested methods, including the baseline bicubic interpolation, offer severely impaired performance. One possible downside of this method is the attenuation of texture details. However, this is also common to nonupscaling denoising algorithms. Also note how noise is amplified by the other super-resolution approaches compared to that of bicubic interpolation and appropriately canceled by our method.

Bicubic	Yang*	Kim*	GR	ANR	Robust	Groundtruth

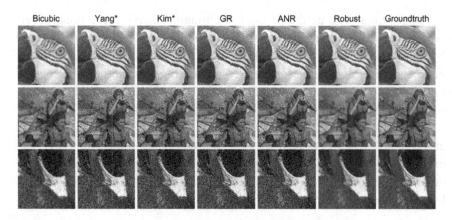

Fig. 3.13 *From top to bottom, details of 2× upscaling of three images corrupted with additive white Gaussian noise with σ = 5, 10, 15, respectively. Note the robustness of the robust method when compared to the other approaches. *Kim et al.'s and Yang et al.'s methods include postprocessing, which is only useful for very low noise levels.*

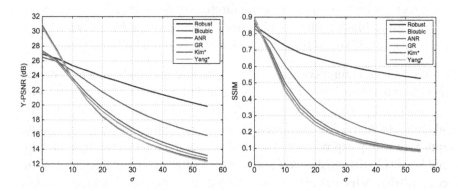

Fig. 3.14 *Y-PSNR (dB) and SSIM for different noise levels σ = 0, 5, ..., 55. Best viewed in color. *Kim et al.'s and Yang et al.'s methods include postprocessing.*

The most relevant results of the objective evaluation can be summarized in Fig. 3.14. Both the PSNR measured on the luminance channel (Y-PSNR) and the Structural Similarity (SSIM) show a much improved performance of the robust high-frequency transfer algorithm when the noise level is high. In the noiseless case, the performance of the method is close to that of ANR and higher than that of the baseline bicubic interpolation (the methods by Yang et al. and Kim et al. use postprocessing and are not suitable for comparison to that respect). As soon as noise corrupts the input images, the robust method clearly provides the best performance (especially in terms of SSIM). We also note the harmful effect of postprocessing with images corrupted by noise, which makes the performance of the postprocessed approaches quickly drop. This validates the earlier observation about the noise amplification by super-resolution approaches in comparison to interpolation-based methods.

Processing Time

On an Intel Xeon W3690, the robust method takes an average 2.1 s/frame to jointly denoise and super-resolve to 720×576 pixels (output size). GR and ANR take average times of 2.1 s and 3.0 s, respectively, and Yang et al.'s method 601.3 s. Kim et al.'s method largely varies from 15 to 170 s with the scene complexity (which becomes higher with increasing noise levels).

3.4 DISCUSSION

We have reviewed three approaches for robust exploitation of high-frequency transfer methods with internal learning. Considering interactive applications, it is important to provide efficient strategies for finding high-frequency examples based on local searches, which is a general requirement for all high-frequency transfer methods. The solution is to limit the scope of the search, either by allowing a compact search window, or by limiting the examples to the in-place location (across several resolution scales). It has been shown that an adaptive selection of the most suitable upscaling and analysis filters can be made based on matching scores. It is also possible to augment this approach by learning the filter selection ahead of their application, which might be achieved by combining the filter selection principle with some of the external learning approaches described in the following chapters. We have also seen a possible way to provide robustness to aliasing to high-frequency transfer methods. The working mechanism is a local exploitation of cross-scale self-similarity, combined with the imposition of priors in high-contrast image regions prone to containing these artifacts. Finally, we have also learned how to modify the cross-scale self-similarity prior in order to automatically select the best possible examples for jointly denoising and complementing with fine detail an initially coarse and noisy version of the desired high-resolution image obtained by interpolation-based upscaling. Given the fact that natural images are sometimes captured with a noticeable amount of noise (especially in video with limited exposure), it is advisable to adopt robust upscaling schemes to ensure the fidelity of the upscaled images with respect to the original scene.

One of the shortcomings in high-frequency transfer, which is common to all internal learning approaches, is the iterative nature of the algorithms to exploit cross-scale self-similarity. In the next chapter, we present an alternative family of techniques, that is, neighbor embedding, which can be naturally used with both internal and external learning. As we shall see, the latter enables single-step upscaling, which has a notable impact when considering real-time or interactive applications with large upscaling factors.

CHAPTER 4

Neighbor Embedding

In this chapter we explore the alternative option of decomposing each image patch as a linear combination of exemplar patches, instead of trying to generalize from a single example as in the previous chapter. In order to do so in a formal way, we can embrace the neighbor embedding framework, which we first explore in general to then focus on the details of its application for super resolution. Whereas the concepts presented in this chapter focus first on an internal learning scenario (examples are extracted from transformations of the input image), the framework is also usable for external learning. However, as we shall see, the application of neighbor embedding for external learning presents important practical shortcomings that lead to the more advanced techniques presented in the next chapters.

4.1 FRAMEWORK

Neighbor embedding, originally presented by Roweis and Saul (2000) is a general framework for compressing the representation of high-dimensional data. Given a high-dimensional datum $x \in \mathbb{R}^m$ and a set of k most similar or Nearest Neighbor data

$$\{\tilde{x}_i\} = \mathrm{NN}(x), \quad i = 1, \ldots, k, \tag{4.1}$$

where $k \ll m$, x can be reconstructed as a linear combination of its nearest neighbors

$$x \approx \sum_{i=1}^{k} w_i \tilde{x}_i. \tag{4.2}$$

The weight w_i represents the relative similarity of the original datum x and the corresponding similar example $\tilde{x}_i$:

$$w_i = \frac{x \cdot \tilde{x}_i}{\sum_{j=1}^{k} x \cdot \tilde{x}_j}. \tag{4.3}$$

Example-Based Super Resolution. http://dx.doi.org/10.1016/B978-0-12-809703-8.00004-6

This definition of the weights ensures that they sum to one:

$$\sum_{i=1}^{k} w_i = \sum_{i=1}^{k} \frac{x \cdot \tilde{x}_i}{\sum_{j=1}^{k} x \cdot \tilde{x}_j} = 1, \tag{4.4}$$

which is actually a very useful constraint to provide robustness, because it enforces that the reconstruction lies in the subspace spanned by the nearest neighbors.

The applicability of this framework for super resolution comes from the fact that neighbor embedding preserves the local geometry of the underlying high-dimensional space. Defining manifolds as topological spaces which are locally Euclidean and assuming that image patches form manifolds in all scales, leads to a straight forward application for super-resolution (Bevilacqua et al., 2012; Chang et al., 2004; Freeman et al., 2002, 2000; Türkan et al., 2014), as described below.

4.1.1 Problem Statement

Let $\tilde{\mathcal{Y}}$ and $\tilde{\mathcal{X}}$ be the manifolds of low-resolution and high-resolution patches, respectively, and s a scalar determining the scale difference between both manifolds (upscaling factor). Under the assumption that most natural image patches are sampled from low-dimensional submanifolds, if a dense sampling of the manifolds is available, then small patches can be reconstructed by their nearest neighbors as follows.

The two manifolds are populated with a large number of exemplar pairs such that, for each low-resolution exemplar $\tilde{y}_i$ in the low-resolution manifold, a high-resolution exemplar $\tilde{x}_i$ in the high-resolution manifold is known.

Now let Y be a low-resolution image for which we wish to estimate a high-resolution version X with an upscaling factor s. The first step consists in dividing the input image into a set of overlapping patches $\{y_p\}$. For each vectorized patch $y_p \in \mathbb{R}^n$, the set of nearest neighbors in $\tilde{\mathcal{Y}}$ is $NN(y_p) = \{\tilde{y}_{p,i}\}$, $i = 1, \ldots, k$.

Once the weights $w_{p,i}$ are defined following Eq. (4.3), the corresponding output vectorized patch $x_p \in \mathbb{R}^m$, where $m = ns^2$, can be reconstructed with Eq. (4.2):

$$x_p = \sum_{i=1}^{k} w_{p,i} \tilde{x}_{p,i}, \qquad (4.5)$$

where $\{\tilde{x}_{p,i}\}$, $i = 1, \ldots, k$ are the high-resolution counterparts to $\{y_{p,i}\}$ in $\tilde{\mathcal{X}}$. Fig. 4.1 illustrates the cross-scale local geometry preservation that enables the application of neighbor embedding for super resolution. The high-resolution image can be reconstructed by overlapping the contributions of the estimated high-resolution patches.

The baseline neighbor-embedding framework presents the following characteristics:

- The local geometry in the manifold is characterized with the weights.
- It is invariant to rotations and re-scalings.
- Robustness is achieved by constraining the reconstruction to lie in the subspace spanned by the nearest neighbors.

The framework thus introduced is general enough to be used for both internal and external learning. In the following we discuss the advantages and shortcomings of each alternative.

4.1.2 Internal vs. External Learning
Internal Learning
When used in internal learning, the input image must be preprocessed in order to generate a sufficiently dense set of exemplar pairs with low-resolution and high-resolution patches. For a desired upscaling factor s, the input image can be first downscaled by the same factor to generate the corresponding low-resolution image. Maintaining the same notation as

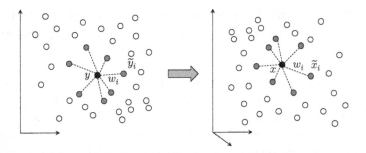

Fig. 4.1 On the left side, a low-resolution (low dimensionality) datum y has been approximated as a weighted combination of its nearest neighbors $\{\tilde{y}_i\}$. On the right side, the same weights can be used on the high-resolution counterparts $\{\tilde{x}_i\}$ of the examples to approximate the high-resolution (high dimensionality) corresponding datum x.

above, that is, X for the high-resolution (desired) image and $Y^{(0)} = Y$ for the low-resolution (observed) image:

$$X^{(1)} = Y^{(0)}, \quad Y^{(1)} = (X^{(1)} * H_d) \downarrow s, \qquad (4.6)$$

where $Y^{(0)}$ is a lower-resolution version of Y, $X^{(0)} = Y$ plays the role of the corresponding high-resolution version with an upscaling factor s and H_d is a downscaling filter to prevent aliasing from appearing in $Y^{(0)}$.

For input images with relatively high resolution, this scheme could also be applied iteratively

$$X^{(n)} = Y^{(n-1)}, \quad Y^{(n)} = (X^{(n)} * H_d) \downarrow s \qquad (4.7)$$

in order to generate an arbitrarily large number of examples and more densely populate the low-resolution and high-resolution exemplar manifolds. However, doing so will also introduce a higher computational cost for the required nearest-neighbor search, so an iterative approach where smaller upscaling factors are iteratively applied until reaching the desired resolution is usually employed. The rationale is that, by doing so, we can keep a relatively sparse-sampled low-resolution manifold thanks to the availability of more meaningful examples, which in turn comes from the cross-scale self-similarity property, that is, better fulfilled for smaller upscaling factors.

As a summary of the two possible modes to apply neighbor embedding with internal learning, we can consider that the computational load vs. quality trade-off will lean us to either:

- Collect a large set of exemplars from many different scales of the input image, thus involving costlier nearest-neighbor searches in a single upscaling step.
- Apply neighbor embedding iteratively under the assumption of enhanced cross-scale self-similarity, which results in reduced nearest-neighbor searches applied during several upscaling steps.

Regardless of whether we attempt to upscale in a single stage with a large set of exemplar pairs, or iteratively with a more compact one, the processing pipeline continues by collecting all the patches in the available low-resolution and high-resolution images (with patch sizes and overlaps differing by the corresponding upscaling factor), thus providing a sampling of the low-resolution and high-resolution manifolds. Then, the nearest-neighbor search and reconstruction steps described above are applied onto each patch and the resulting high-resolution patches are overlapped to produce the output image.

External Learning

When applying neighbor embedding with external learning, the iterative option actually makes little sense: The availability of a large amount of training exemplar pairs means that, in order to obtain compact, yet meaningful, samples for the image (at the current scale) we have to determine a suitable subset of the entire database, which intuitively will impose a computational cost similar to that of applying nearest-neighbor searches on the entire set of exemplars.

Thus, the natural way to apply neighbor embedding and the one that has generated a large degree of attention in the literature is to collect a large set of low-resolution and high-resolution examples in the form of paired overcomplete dictionaries during an offline stage (Bevilacqua et al., 2012; Chang et al., 2004). Overcomplete dictionaries are dictionaries where the number of exemplars or manifold samples is much larger than the dimensionality of the underlying sampled manifold. During the testing or online stage, fast (approximate) nearest-neighbor search approaches are required in order to efficiently apply neighbor embedding.

An alternative and costlier solution is to jointly obtain the optimal number of nearest-neighbors within the low-resolution dictionary and their weights, which can be accomplished by means of the imposition of sparsity constraints. Let $\mathbf{D}_l$ and $\mathbf{D}_h$ be the low-resolution and high-resolution overcomplete dictionaries obtained from a large set of exemplar pairs. Each dictionary can be expressed as a *fat* matrix where each column is a vectorized exemplar. The joint optimization results in a well-known problem that can be solved, for example, by means of Orthogonal Matching Pursuit (Cai & Wang, 2011):

$$w^* = \arg \min_{w} \|y - \mathbf{D}_l w\|_2^2 + \lambda_s \|w\|_1. \tag{4.8}$$

In this optimization problem, sparsity is enforced by means of the relaxation of the $L0$-norm of the weight vector w to a more efficiently computable $L1$-norm, and the corresponding regularization constant λ_s balancing the relative contributions of the data-fidelity and regularization terms. As we shall see in the next chapter, this costly approach can be optimized by using thinner dictionaries that guarantee generalization, leading to sparse coding approaches.

4.2 EXTENSIONS

The goal of this section is to present two possible ways to extend the general formulation in the neighbor embedding framework. The first extension focuses on internal learning with enlarged sets of examples, whereas the second one is presented with both internal learning and external learning scenarios in mind, thus bridging the gap between internal and external learning.

4.2.1 Multiphase Neighbor Embeddings

One way to finely tune the neighbor embedding framework results is from paying special attention to the example generation step. Note that, when generating the low-resolution part of the exemplar pairs by means of the downscaling operator, a large part of the information contained in the input image is thrown away by the antialiasing filter H_d. This filter typically presents a polyphase implementation, such that, for each output pixel in a sequential processing order, a filter with a different phase is circularly applied. This behavior is illustrated in Fig. 4.2, where a one-dimensional signal is downscaled by a factor $s = 4/3$, thus resulting in a signal with a length 3/4 of the original one. Because image data are two-dimensional, the number of different filter curves for a given downscaling factor is actually quadratical with respect to the one-dimensional case.

Taking into account the details of the polyphase downscaling implementation, an alternative approach to enlarge the number of available examples, while still relying on the cross-scale self-similarity, is to consider the different phases from the downscaling antialiasing filter. This approach

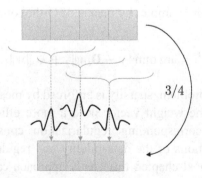

Fig. 4.2 *The samples of a one-dimensional are resampled to 3/4 of the original length. The polyphase filter consists of three different curves that are circularly selected for each output sample.*

has been discussed in detail by Türkan et al. (2013). This approach is interesting because it poses a relatively novel question. It is well-known that different patches in high-resolution collapse to the same appearance when downscaled, due to the effect of the antialiasing filter and the decimation step. This algorithm presents an alternative view of the problem, illustrated in Fig. 4.3. Given a sliding window on the patches in the high-resolution version of the image, the corresponding low-resolution patches can be determined through small variations resulting from the selection of one of the polyphase filters.

Pipeline

An iterative algorithm exploiting the enriched multiphase examples can be envised by enlarging the input patches one pixel at a time. The interesting aspect of this algorithm is that it does not reconstruct the entire image until all patches have been iteratively upscaled to the target resolution. Let us take a look at the pipeline for upscaling factor $s = 2$ in more detail:

1. Starting from a 3×3 patch in the input image, the first iteration estimates its appearance with a resolution of 4×4 pixels, that is, $s_1 = 4/3$ at the patch level. The examples for this stage are built from the input image by downscaling by s_1, that is, generating a set of 3^2 multiphase images with $3/4$ the original size along each dimension.
2. Starting from the 4×4 patch from the previous stage, the second iteration estimates its appearance with a resolution of 5×5 pixels, that is,

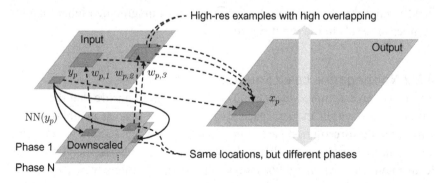

Fig. 4.3 Neighbor low-resolution samples obtained from different phases in the same location in the low-resolution downscaled images correspond to highly overlapping patches from the input image, that is, the high-resolution examples.

$s_2 = 5/4$ at the patch level. The examples are built by downscaling the input image by s_2, that is, generating a set of 4^2 multiphase images with $4/5$ the original size along each dimension.

3. Starting from the 5×5 patch, the third and last iteration estimates the 6×6 patch corresponding to the desired upscaling factor $s = 2$. The last iteration's upscaling factor is thus $s_3 = 6/5$ and the examples are built by downscaling the input by s_2, that is, generating a set of 5^2 multiphase images with $5/6$ the original size along each dimension.

In all steps, the sum-to-one constraint imposed to determine the weights of each nearest neighbor ensures that the reconstructed patches lie in the subspaces spanned by the high-resolution counterpart of the low-resolution nearest neighbors. Once all 3×3 patches of the input image are upscaled to 6×6 patches, the high-resolution image is reconstructed by averaging the contributions of the overlapping upscaled patches and optionally applying postprocessing based on iterative back-projection (Irani & Peleg, 1991).

Complexity

Similarly to high-frequency transfer, the iterative exploitation of cross-scale self-similarity imposes an increasing running time with each stage. For an exhaustive nearest-neighbor search, the first stage requires in the order of $p^2 \cdot \frac{n(p+1)}{p} = p(p + 1)n$ searches per patch, where n is the total number of pixels in the input image, p the side of the original patch, that is, 3 in the pipeline described above, the first factor is the number of different downscaled image phases and the second factor is the approximate number of possible patch positions in each downscaled image. For the last iteration, this number grows up to $(p + 2)^2 \cdot \frac{p+3}{p+2} = (p + 2)(p + 3)n$, which results in a total number of searches about two orders of magnitude higher than the number of pixels in the input image.

4.2.2 Nonnegative Least Squares

So far we have assumed the sum-to-one condition to ensure that the reconstruction lies within the subspace spanned by the nearest neighbor atoms within the high-resolution part of the dictionary. In this section we describe an alternative criterion to obtain the weights of the nearest neighbors that leads to an enhanced neighbor embedding for applications were an external overcomplete dictionary of low-resolution and high-resolution exemplar pairs may be available as in Freeman et al. (2000), Chang et al. (2004), and Bevilacqua et al. (2012).

Features

Neighbor embedding can naturally be carried out in a feature space: low-resolution and high-resolution patches can obviously be represented by vectors of features computed from the raw luminance values of the pixels of the patch (Chang et al., 2004). The role of the feature representation is two-fold:

- On the one hand, to convey the most relevant part of the low-resolution information and provide a good approximation suitable for the high-resolution patch reconstruction.
- On the other, to possibly enforce the similarity between the low-resolution and high-resolution patch structures, which better aligns with the local geometry invariance of the neighbor-embedding framework.

It is common for many existing methods in the literature to preprocess the input images according to the idea that the low part of the spectrum of the low-resolution patches is the most helpful information to learn the low-resolution to high-resolution correspondences. In the original neighbor embedding algorithm by Chang et al. (2004) and many follow-ups (Bevilacqua et al., 2012; Zeyde et al., 2012), features derived from the first and second-order gradients are taken into account. Regarding the representation of the high-resolution patches, a common solution is to directly use the raw luminance values of the high-resolution version of the training images, possibly after contrast normalization or mean removal. Because the output of the method is an image, it is natural that the output of the regression stage for each patch directly represents the corresponding part of the output image. Floating low-resolution patches, that is, patches with their mean luminance subtracted, can also be useful as input features, as discussed by Bevilacqua et al. (2012).

Method

Nonnegative least squares (Hanson & Lawson, 1974) can be used to provide the weights of the nearest neighbors when relaxing the sum-to-one condition to a nonnegativity one:

$$w^* = \arg\min_{w} \|y - \mathbf{NN}(y)w\|_2^2 \quad \text{s.t.} \quad w \geq 0. \tag{4.9}$$

Abusing notation, $\mathbf{NN}(y)$ refers to the matrix obtained by stacking, column-wise all vectorized nearest neighbors of the input x. The use of the nonnegativity constraint allows for considering more neighbors for the embedding stage than the ones accepted by the sum-to-one constraint. In turn, the larger set of examples results in an improved reconstruction accuracy. The pipeline of the method exploiting the nonnegativity constraint consists in:

1. Divide the input image Y into small overlapping floating patches $\{y_p\}$.
2. Obtain the nearest neighbors of each patch in the low-resolution part of the overcomplete dictionary or example database $\{NN(y_p)\}$.
3. Determine the weights $\{w_p\}$ of all patches through Eq. (4.9).
4. Reconstruct the high-resolution patches $\{x_p\}$ through Eq. (4.5).
5. Reconstruct the super-resolved image X by averaging the contributions of the overlapping patches.

4.3 PERFORMANCE

We focus on the performance of the nonnegative least squares neighbor embedding (NNLS-NE). This choice responds to the fact that this method provides a convenient bridge between the internal learning and external learning approaches discussed in the next chapters. We first review some configuration details and then compare measure its performance.

4.3.1 Configuration

Similarly to the case of high-frequency transfer, neighbor embedding also benefits from the application of iterative back-projection (Bevilacqua et al., 2012; Irani & Peleg, 1991; Türkan et al., 2013; J. Yang et al., 2010) as a postprocessing stage:

$$X^{(n+1)} := X^{(n)} + H_u * ((Y - (X^{(n)} * H_d) \downarrow s) \uparrow s) \qquad (4.10)$$

with H_u an upscaling interpolation filter, H_d an antialiasing downscaling filter, and s the upscaling factor.

A reasonable size for the patches in the input image is 3×3 pixels, with sliding window (vertical and horizontal strides equal to 1). We can also enforce that the upscaling is performed in a single step. In this case, the size and the overlap degree of the high-resolution patches depend on the magnification factor s, for example, the high-resolution patch has dimensions $3s \times 3s$ pixels with a vertical and horizontal stride equal to s. Large overlaps provide smoother reconstructed images with a reduced amount of reconstruction noise due to the cancellation of the disagreements by means of averaging.

Table 4.1 Performance in Reconstruction PSNR (dB) and Size of Example Database for Single-Step Upscaling Using Nonnegative Least Squares With Internal and External Learning					
		Internal		External	
Image	s	PSNR	Examples	PSNR	Examples
Baby	4	27.95	~2k	30.47	~100k
Bird	3	27.72	~2k	31.40	~250k
Woman	2	27.79	~15k	30.67	~500k

Internal vs. External Learning

Table 4.1 shows the effect of the database selection for upscaling three images from the Set5 dataset. The Set5 is a dataset composed by five images of varied (small) sizes which contain a high amount of sharp structures and textures. Obviously, applying super resolution in a single step with internal learning results in bad performance, because the cross-scale self-similarity property does not hold for large upscaling factors. In contrast, the use of a large amount of samples of the underlying low-resolution and high-resolution manifolds with external examples allows direct upscaling in a single step. Naturally, the selection of a large amount of examples will be beneficial in terms of reconstruction accuracy, but also computationally costly, because nearest neighbor searches in a large database have to be carried on for each patch. The external database, which is used in the rest of experiments, is constructed by simply collecting patches from the low-resolution (downscaled) versions of a set of images and their high-resolution (original) counterparts.

4.3.2 Benchmark

The nonnegative least square algorithm with iterative back-projection post-processing (NNLS-NE) is compared to the original locally linear embedding algorithm (LLE-NE) by Chang et al. (2004). Table 4.2 summarizes the results for all images in Set5 and three different magnification factors, including the output PSNR and the running time in seconds.

When comparing both algorithms, we should note that LLE-NE includes gradient-based features, whereas NNLS-NE uses mean-subtracted patches and includes postprocessing. In general, the selected configuration in NNLS-NE provides notably higher performance, but in the absence of the iterative back-projection step, the performance of both methods is comparable.

Table 4.2 Performance in Terms of PSNR (dB) and Running Time (s) of Locally Linear Embedding (LLE-NE) and Nonnegative Least Squares Neighbor Embedding With Iterative Back-Projection (NNLS-NE) for 2×, 3×, and 4× Upscaling With All Images From Set5 (Best Results in Bold)					
		LLE-NE		NNLS-NE	
Image	s	PSNR	Time	PSNR	Time
Baby	2	33.42	171	**34.64**	30
Bird	2	32.94	55	**34.69**	9
Butterfly	2	25.90	38	**27.54**	9
Head	2	32.34	72	**32.88**	9
Woman	2	29.43	57	**30.91**	8
Baby	3	31.00	58	**32.44**	14
Bird	3	29.71	47	**31.37**	5
Butterfly	3	22.58	17	**24.31**	5
Head	3	30.82	34	**31.46**	6
Woman	3	26.45	18	**27.98**	6
Baby	4	29.27	43	**30.62**	11
Bird	4	27.37	11	**28.99**	4
Butterfly	4	20.50	18	**22.05**	4
Head	4	29.57	13	**30.26**	4
Woman	4	24.25	9	**25.66**	3

4.4 DISCUSSION

In this chapter we have reviewed the neighbor-embedding framework for super resolution. As we have seen, it can use just a given input image or a collected database of images, thus bridging the gap between internal learning and external learning methods. The goal is to regress the appearance of the high-resolution patches through the translation of the local geometry of the low-resolution patch manifold.

Neighbor embedding is a powerful framework for internal learning super resolution when applied iteratively. However, the iterative application of small upscaling factors might render the computational cost too high for some applications, especially if aiming at real time. This problem is common to the two approaches for internal learning that we have reviewed. We have also seen how external learning provides single-step upscaling, but it is, again, computationally costly due to the requirement of determining the nearest neighbors for each patch out of a large example database.

In the next chapters we delve into more efficient approaches for exploiting external example databases toward single-step upscaling with reduced computational cost.

CHAPTER 5

Sparse Coding

The core idea behind sparse signal representation, or sparse coding, is that linear relationships between signals can be precisely reconstructed from their low-dimensional projections (Lee, Battle, Raina, & Ng, 2007). The application of sparse signal representation to super resolution was first proposed by J. Yang, Wright, Huang, and Ma (2008) and has been a very active research topic (Lu, Yuan, Yan, Yuan, & Li, 2012; J. Yang et al., 2010; Zhang, Gao, Tao, & Li, 2012).

In this chapter we first review the general sparse coding framework, including the data model and some dictionary training approaches. Then we focus on an extension toward adaptivity based on the Naive Bayes Nearest Neighbor framework by McCann and Lowe (2012). Finally, we provide some implementation notes for the adaptive extension and analyze its performance relative to nonadaptive techniques.

5.1 SUPER RESOLUTION MODEL

Let X be a high-resolution image that can be analyzed into overlapping patches x and Y the low-resolution counterpart from which we extract patches y based on the known model or reconstruction constraint

$$Y = (X * H) \downarrow s, \tag{5.1}$$

where $\downarrow s$ is a decimator operator (with downscaling factor s) and H is the transfer function modeling blur. As expected, for a given Y, recovering X remains an ill-posed problem because many high-resolution images comply with the reconstruction constraint.

5.1.1 Sparse Reconstruction

A sparse coding super-resolution approach, with an inference pipeline, such as the one illustrated in Fig. 5.1, solves this ill-posed problem by assuming a sparsity prior

$$x \approx D_h \alpha \quad \text{for some } \alpha \in \mathbb{R}^k \text{with } \|\alpha\|_0 \ll k, \tag{5.2}$$

where D_h is an overcomplete dictionary containing vectorized high-resolution patches, or atoms, k is the number of atoms in D_h, and α is

Example-Based Super Resolution. http://dx.doi.org/10.1016/B978-0-12-809703-8.00005-8

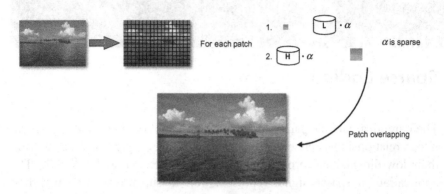

For each patch
1. ▦
2. [H] · α

[L] · α
α is sparse

Patch overlapping

Fig. 5.1 Sparse reconstruction at work. For each patch, a sparse decomposition is computed as a linear combination of a small number of entries in a low-resolution dictionary. The high-resolution reconstruction is obtained by applying the same mixing coefficients onto the corresponding high-resolution dictionary. The high-resolution image can be computed by combining the contributions of each patch.

the sparse representation of x with a small amount of nonzero entries ($\ll k$). In order to recover x, the sparse representation α must actually be computed from the observable low-resolution patches y with respect to a dictionary containing the corresponding vectorized low-resolution patches D_l and possibly using a feature transformation F:

$$\min \|\alpha\|_0 \quad \text{s.t.} \quad \|FD_l\alpha - Fy\|_2^2 \leq \epsilon. \tag{5.3}$$

This optimization problem can be rephrased, using Lagrange multipliers, with the equivalent formulation proposed by J. Yang et al. (2008):

$$\min_{\alpha} \|FD_l\alpha - Fy\|_2^2 + \lambda \|\alpha\|_0, \tag{5.4}$$

where the regularization parameter λ provides a trade-off between the sparsity and accuracy of the found solution. Because patches extracted from an image are commonly sampled with a certain overlap, the optimization problem in Eq. (5.4) can be redefined in such a way that adjacent patches are compatible:

$$\alpha^* = \min_{\alpha} \|\tilde{D}\alpha - \tilde{y}\|_2^2 + \lambda \|\alpha\|_0, \tag{5.5}$$

where

$$\tilde{D} = \begin{bmatrix} FD_l \\ PD_h \end{bmatrix} \quad \text{and} \quad \tilde{y} = \begin{bmatrix} Fy \\ w \end{bmatrix}. \tag{5.6}$$

P describes the overlap region between the current patch and the previously reconstructed high-resolution image (raster order) and w describes the previously reconstructed values for the overlap region. After solving the optimization problem in Eq. (5.5), we can reconstruct the high-resolution patches by applying the sparse coding as

$$x = D_h \alpha^*. \tag{5.7}$$

5.1.2 Dictionary Training

The simplest way to obtain the dictionaries needed for sparse reconstruction is to directly extract raw patches from the training images as in J. Yang et al. (2008), similarly as in neighbor embedding. The problem of this approach is that large dictionaries will substantially increase the computational cost of the online optimization problem in Eq. (5.5). J. Yang et al. (2010) show how computational time grows linearly with the dictionary size, thus rendering neighbor embedding approaches too costly for real-world problems. J. Yang et al. (2010) tackle this problem by using sparse coding techniques. The goal is to obtain a still overcomplete, yet more compact, set of *basis vectors*, able to extract high level patterns of the input unlabeled data (Lee et al., 2007), thus resulting in a sparse dictionary.

Let $T = [t_1, t_2, \ldots, t_n] \in \mathbb{R}^{m \times n}$ be a collection of examples or training patches and $D = [d_1, d_2, \ldots, d_k] \in \mathbb{R}^{m \times k}$ an overcomplete sparse dictionary containing all the patch bases. Now let $S = [s_1, s_2, \ldots, s_n] \in \mathbb{R}^{k \times n}$ be a matrix with all the coefficients for all training patches in T. The dictionary entries weighted by these coefficients should best approximate T, thus we can use the objective function

$$\min_{D,S} \|T - DS\|_2^2 + \lambda_s \|S\|_1 \quad s.t. \quad \|d_i\|_2^2 \le 1, \quad i = 1, 2, \ldots, k, \tag{5.8}$$

where λ_s is a regularization parameter, $\|S\|_1$ enforces sparsity of the decomposition, and $\|d_i\|^2$ removes scale ambiguity. The formulation in Eq. (5.8) has been broadly studied, and despite not being convex in both D and S, it is convex in one of them, while the other is fixed, as shown by Lee et al. (2007). Consequently, in order to minimize Eq. (5.8), an alternate iterative scheme is used, that is, updating one variable while the other is fixed until convergence.

Joint Training

For super resolution, a pair of training data matrices, T_h and T_l with high-resolution and low-resolution data points or patches, respectively, is required. A possible option is to jointly train two dictionaries so that the sparse representation of the high-resolution datapoints is the same as the sparse representation of the corresponding low-resolution datapoints. With that purpose, the following minimization can be performed:

$$\min_{\{D_h,D_l,S\}} \frac{1}{L_h} \|T_h - D_hS\|_2^2 + \frac{1}{L_l} \|T_l - D_lS\|_2^2 + \lambda_s \left(\frac{1}{L_h} + \frac{1}{L_l}\right) \|S\|_1, \quad (5.9)$$

where L_h and L_l are the dimensionalities of the high-resolution and low-resolution patches, respectively.

Single-Scale Training

Another option to obtain the dictionaries is to first obtain the low-resolution dictionary out of the corresponding training examples, or features thereof, and also extract the sparse coefficients for all examples (contained in matrix S):

$$\min_{D_l,S} \|T_l - D_lS\|_2^2 + \lambda_s \|S\|_1 \quad \text{s.t.} \quad \|d_{l,i}\|_2^2 \leq 1, \quad i = 1, \ldots, k. \quad (5.10)$$

Alternatively, the K-SVD algorithm by Aharon et al. (2006) can also be used to compute the low-resolution dictionary. Then, using the sparse mixing coefficients S, the high-resolution dictionary can be computed in closed form as:

$$\min_{D_h} \|T_h - D_hS\|_F^2 \iff D_h = T_hS^\top \left(SS^\top\right)^{-1}, \quad (5.11)$$

where the subscript F in the norm indicates the Frobenius norm. Obviously, this procedure can also be employed starting with the high-resolution dictionary, but doing so will result in a noticeably higher computational cost due to the iterative nature of the first step.

The performance of all learning-based super-resolution methods depends strongly on the contents of the training dataset. In neighbor-embedding approaches like (J. Yang et al., 2008), the dictionary is built by randomly sampling raw patches from a large set of images, regardless of the image to be recovered, hence relying on gathering sufficiently diverse patches so that they can generalize for any patch to be super-resolved. In the neighbor-embedding super-resolution work of Gao, Zhang, Tao, and Li (2012), a clustering in the training set is performed based on geometrical structure of patches. The k-Nearest Neighbor (k-NN) query of the input low-resolution patch is then carried out within the closest cluster, thus showing some adaptive behavior. Nevertheless, the patches to be included in the clustering are also randomly selected out of a larger set of training patches. More recent follow-up works (Lu et al., 2012; J. Yang et al., 2010) keep using the same random sampling strategy during training, although the raw patches are compressed into sparse dictionaries without losing generalization.

5.2 ADAPTIVE EXTENSION

In all cases, the contents of D_h and D_l are ultimately determined by the contents of the training examples T_h and T_l. Thus, the composition of these subsets is of capital importance for the whole super-resolution process. In this section we review an alternative that adaptively builds T_h and T_l from the training images based on the contents of the input low-resolution image Y.

This approach includes a stage which adaptively selects square regions in the training images which better represent each of the input image patches, without doing any manual image preselection. The key idea is to extract training patch pairs only from square regions likely to contain similar structure and texture to the ones present in the input image. By doing so, the training of the dictionary, in any of the forms described above, can be carried on from a set of training pairs T_h and T_l adapted to the structures and textures of the input image Y.

5.2.1 Training Region Selection

Each training image I_T is split into square regions R of size L_R. The problem is, given a patch y, find its training texture region R. Assuming a uniform prior over all regions R (all of them are equally likely to be used), the selection can be based on a Maximum Likelihood (ML) decision rule:

$$\hat{R} = \arg\max_R p(R \mid y) = \arg\max_R p(y \mid R). \tag{5.12}$$

Let $\{f\} = f_1, f_2, \ldots, f_n$ denote some descriptors or features extracted from patch y (further details about useful descriptors are given in Section 5.3.1). We can use the Naive Bayes assumption, that is, that descriptors are independent, identically distributed:

$$p(y \mid R) = p(f_1, f_2, \ldots, f_n \mid R) = \prod_{i=1}^{n} p(f_i \mid R). \tag{5.13}$$

Then, the log-likelihood reads:

$$\hat{R} = \arg\max_R \sum_{i=1}^{n} \log p(f_i \mid R). \tag{5.14}$$

This decision requires computing the probability density $p(f \mid R)$, which can be obtained through a nearest-neighbor (NN) approximation of a Parzen density estimation $p_{NN}(f \mid R)$, as proposed by Boiman, Shechtman, and Irani (2008).

For that purpose, let $\{f^R\} = f_1^R, f_2^R, \ldots, f_L^R$ be all the descriptors of a region R, where f_j^R is the jth descriptor. The Parzen kernel

$$K(f_i - f_j^R) = \exp\left(-\frac{1}{2\sigma^2}\left\|f_i - f_j^R\right\|^2\right) \tag{5.15}$$

yields negligible values for very distant descriptors because K exponentially decreases with distance. Therefore, using only the r NN of descriptor f will accurately approximate the Parzen estimation:

$$p_{NN}(f_i \mid R) = \frac{1}{L}\sum_{j=1}^{r} K(f_i - jNN_R(f_i)) \tag{5.16}$$

In Boiman et al. (2008) a minor decrease in performance is observed when using as little as $r = 1$ NN compared to the full Parzen window estimation, whereas this choice considerably simplifies Eq. (5.14):

$$\hat{R} = \arg\min_R \sum_{i=1}^{n} \|f_i - NN_R(f_i)\|^2 . \tag{5.17}$$

Solving Eq. (5.17) requires calculating the distance from the patch to all existing regions in the training dataset. This might be computationally prohibitive because usual training sets can contain hundreds of images which translates in a number of regions in the order of thousands. Recent research in Naive Bayes Nearest-Neighbor (NBNN) classifiers proposed local NBNN (McCann & Lowe, 2012), which solves this problem by only exploring the local neighborhood of each descriptor f_i. The runtime grows with the log of the number of categories rather than linearly as in Boiman et al. (2008), which results in sensitive speed-ups for large numbers of categories (the results in McCann and Lowe (2012) show a 100× speed-up for 256 categories) while still outperforming the original method by Boiman et al. (2008) in classification accuracy.

Let R be some region and $\bar{R}$ the set of all other regions. If we reformulate the NBNN updates as adjustments to the posterior log-odds, the alternative decision rule will be

$$\hat{R} = \arg\max_R \sum_{i=1}^{n} \log\frac{P(f_i \mid R)}{P(f_i \mid \bar{R})} + \log\frac{P(R)}{P(\bar{R})}. \tag{5.18}$$

Again, the prior can be dropped if we assume uniform over R. The benefit of this alternative formulation as log-odds increments is that we can select the region posteriors which give a positive contribution on the sum in Eq. (5.18). Thus, the main improvements of using local NBNN are:

- Only using the closest member from the regions whose descriptors are within the k-nearest neighbors of each f_i
- Modeling the distance to the rest of the regions $P(f_i \mid \overline{R})$ as the distance to the $k+1$ nearest neighbor.

After finding a region R for every patch y, we can proceed by sampling patches of size L_p with a certain overlap inside the selected regions and include them in high-resolution and low-resolution training sets T_h and T_l, which will be used for training the sparse dictionaries as described above. A summary including further implementation details can be found in Algorithm 2.

Algorithm 2 Adaptive Training (Y, R)

Require: A Nearest Neighbor index containing all descriptors from all regions, queried by NN(d, *#neighbors*).

Require: Region lookup function REGION(*descriptor*) that retrieves the region to which *descriptor* belongs to.

Require: Sampling patches function SAMPPATCHES(*Region*) which extracts patches with a certain overlap.

for all patches $y \in Y$ **do**

  for all descriptors $d_i \in y$ **do**

    $\{p_1, p_2, \ldots, p_{k+1}\} \leftarrow NN(d_i, k+1)$

    for all regions R found in the k nearest neighbors **do**

      $dist_R = \min_{\{p_j | \text{REGION}(p_j)\}} \|d_i - p_j\|^2$

    end for

    $totals[R] \leftarrow totals[R] + dist_R - dist_B$

  end for

  $Selected[y] \leftarrow \arg\min_R totals[R]$

end for

for all Selected unique regions **do**

  $T \leftarrow$ SAMPPATCHES$(Selected[R])$

end for

return T

Fig. 5.2 Appearance of 50 × 50 regions extracted from a set of training images. From left to right and top to bottom: rope, stones, sand, bear fur, tree bark, hair. Super-resolution performance can be improved by selecting a meaningful set of regions for every input image.

5.2.2 Region Rejection

Some regions extracted from the training images might not be useful because they do not contain a relevant amount of patches with high-frequency information (e.g., regions with blurry unfocused backgrounds or uniform colors). In order to reject these regions, we can, for example, apply a high-pass filter whose cut-off frequency is related to the magnification factor s. Intuitively, we should require a broader spectrum when a higher magnification factor is selected, according to the cut-off frequency $f_c = 1 - \frac{\beta}{s}$, where β can be used to weigh the impact of the second addend. The energy per pixel in the filtered region R', can be defined as $E = \left\| R' \right\|_2^2 / L_R^2$. Based on this measure, we can reject a region R when its energy E is lower than a given threshold ε. Some examples of selected regions are shown in Fig. 5.2.

5.3 APPLICATION

In this section we first review some implementation details for methods based on sparse coding, including the adaptive extensions described above, and then proceed with some application examples. Of special interest is the multiview scenario, where the adaptive approach provides a mechanism to exploit cross-view redundancies, even without specific knowledge about the geometry of the scene or the calibration of the multicamera rig.

5.3.1 Feature Space

Many feature representations have been proposed in the literature for boosting super resolution, according to the criteria that mid- and high-frequency are the most useful frequency bands when learning low-resolution to high-resolution patch correspondences. In neighbor embedding, Freeman et al. (2000) used a simple high-pass filter in order to obtain the low-resolution patch information closer in frequency to the one to be predicted in the high-resolution patch. Later on, J. Sun, Zheng, Tao, and Shum (2003) used Gaussian derivative filters to also extract the high frequency information of the low-resolution patches. In the same direction, Chang et al. (2004) and J. Yang et al. (2008) used concatenated first- and second-order gradients.

In general, different tasks shall benefit from different types of feature descriptors. Without focusing on an exhaustive search for optimal features, in the following, we review some reasonable choices:

- Concatenated first- and second-order gradients of luminance as the F_l feature transform for patches in D_l, following Chang et al. (2004) and J. Yang et al. (2008).
- Centered luminance values in D_h, considering the constraint for the descriptors to be easily reversible to pixel values. In this feature representation we subtract to every luminance value the mean of the patch luminance (i.e., eliminating the DC component from the patch). Although keeping the same descriptors as in D_l would be desirable to make a more consistent descriptor space, a direct reversion step is not feasible for gradient descriptors.
- Dense Scale Invariant Feature Transform (SIFT) descriptors (Lowe, 2004). We can use SIFT or equivalent descriptors for the region selection stage. Such descriptors typically show improved resilience to changes in image scale and rotation, and they are robust to changes in illumination, noise, and viewpoint. Using dense SIFT extraction instead of the original SIFT detector we can enforce a certain number of features per patch.

5.3.2 Performance
In this section, we verify the performance gain of the adaptive method when compared to classic sparse-reconstruction and neighbor-embedding alternatives.

Training and Testing Sets
In order to assess the effectivity of the adaptive training scheme, two different testing scenarios and a single training set are described here. The training dataset for the adaptive approach comprises the training images

provided in the Berkeley Segmentation dataset *BSD500*[1] composed by 200 generic images with a resolution of 380 × 420 pixels and 60 images from the INRIA 4d repository[2] consisting of captures of four different scenes (karate, stick, children, dog) as seen from 16 different cameras. The testing scenarios are

(a) six randomly selected generic images from the Berkeley testing dataset (referred to as *Berkeley*)
(b) The 16th view of the four different multiview scenes plus 2 images from different time frames and cameras (referred to as *multiview*).

With these two testing sets we can validate that the adaptive method improves performance for generic images by just selecting optimal training regions and, most interestingly, that the adaptive method leads to effectively exploiting correlated visual information in appropriate regions within the training images when dealing with common scenarios as multiview recordings or multiframe information in video sequences.

As accustomed, for each testing image, we set the full resolution version as ground-truth, then we downscale it using bicubic interpolation by the 2× and 3× magnification factors and finally apply the different super-resolution algorithms to restore it to its original resolution. Using the ground-truth image, we compute the luminance peak signal-to-noise-ratio (PSNR) and the Structural Similarity (SSIM) index, a quality measure based on the degradation of structural information (Z. Wang, Bovik, Sheikh, & Simoncelli, 2004). In the case of the *multiview* testing images, the original images have been predownscaled to have a ground-truth resolution of 800 × 600 to get rid of demosaicing artifacts, and we match the resolution of the INRIA 4d repository training images to that of the input (i.e., different for each magnification factor) so that none of the training images from the INRIA 4d repository has higher resolution than the *multiview* input images.

Comparison With Other Methods
The adaptive method is compared with two classic super-resolution approaches: the neighbor-embedding method by Chang et al. (2004) and the sparse-coding one by J. Yang et al. (2010). In the implementation of the adaptive method, dictionaries are adaptively trained with the above described approach and used with J. Yang et al. (2010). The direct

[1]http://www.eecs.berkeley.edu/Research/Projects/CS/vision/grouping/resources.html
[2]http://4drepository.inrialpes.fr/pages/home

Table 5.1 Average Results From *Multiview* and *Berkeley* Testing Scenarios (First Row Is PSNR in dB and Second Row Is SSIM. Best Results in Bold)

	Neighbor Embedding		Sparse Coding		Sparse Adaptive	
	2×	3×	2×	3×	2×	3×
Multiview	38.060	34.195	40.772	36.089	**41.276**	**36.487**
	0.9667	0.9310	0.9774	0.9504	**0.980**	**0.952**
Berkeley	27.707	24.781	29.853	26.262	**30.191**	**26.413**
	0.8544	0.7430	0.9099	0.8121	**0.9143**	**0.8149**

comparison is therefore explicitly showing the improvement obtained by adaptivity.

When testing with neighbor embedding, the parameters and reduced training set recommended in the original paper are used, adding an additional training image from the INRIA 4d repository in order to keep a fair ratio between generic images and those correlated with *multiview* in the training set. For the adaptive method, the square region size is fixed to $L_R = 50$ pixels, the patch size to $L_p = 6$ pixels, and the k-NN search of the local NBNN is set to $k = 10$. For both the baseline sparse-coding method and the adaptive one, the same 260 training images have been used, selecting in both cases, 100,000 patch pairs and compressing them into sparse dictionaries D_h and D_l of 512 elements.

Table 5.1 summarizes the obtained results, reporting the PSNR and SSIM average values for the different testing sets and magnification factors. Fig. 5.3 offers visual results for one image of each testing set.

Comparing adaptive sparse coding to the neighbor embedding method by Chang et al. (2004), the visual improvements are easily noticeable: the adaptive method is clearly super-resolving finer details resulting in sharper images. The objective PSNR and SSIM results support this qualitative visual impression.

With respect to the baseline sparse-coding method by J. Yang et al. (2010), careful visual inspection shows that ringing artifacts along the edges are mostly suppressed and certain edges are sharper in the adaptive improvement. In quantitative results, the latter outperforms (J. Yang et al., 2010) in both PSNR and SSIM for the two magnification factors tested and in both testing set-ups. We observe larger improvements in performance when training and testing images are related (*multiview* test, 0.504 dB PSNR

Fig. 5.3 *Reconstructed high-resolution images (magnification factor 2×) from Berkeley (left) and multiview (right) testing sets. From top to bottom: Ground truth image, neighbor embedding, sparse coding, and adaptive sparse coding.*

gain for $2\times$ magnification factor), but there is also significant improvement for generic testing images (*Berkeley* test, 0.338 dB PSNR improvement for $2\times$ magnification factor). We can attribute the better performance to the fact that the image-adapted subsets T_h and T_l can represent the data more accurately, and that this adaptation is stronger whenever testing and some training image regions are correlated.

5.4 DISCUSSION

This chapter has presented classic sparse coding as an improvement over neighbor embedding, including a powerful extension which focuses on adaptively selecting improved examples for dictionary training. Observing the fact that images usually contain a nonpredictable group of different elements with their characteristic textures and edges (e.g., grass, rocks, fur, sand), adaptive sparse coding first divides the training images into subimage regions of sizes that preserve texture and structure consistency. The best-representing region for each input low-resolution patch in the input image is found through an efficient Bayesian selection stage. In this selection process, SIFT or similar descriptors are densely extracted for both the input low-resolution patches and the training regions. Then, local Naive Bayes Nearest-Neighbor can be used to efficiently handle the potentially high number of different regions in the training dataset. The resulting adapted subset of patches is then compressed, using the classic sparse coding techniques and used to recover high-resolution images by exploiting the sparsity prior without any modification to the decomposition and reconstruction pipeline. Both the classic sparse coding scheme and the adaptive extension clearly outperform classic neighbor embedding for generic images. The improvement of the adaptive extension is accentuated when training regions related to the testing images exist within the training dataset, thus making this extension also suitable for applications where these conditions are met (e.g., video sequences, multiview scenarios, or metadata-tagged images).

On the downside, sparse coding techniques involve a costly sparse decomposition of each input patch as a linear combination of the atoms in the low-resolution dictionary. Even more so, the adaptive approach needs to compute a dictionary for each frame! Even though recent improvements of classic sparse coding have already been presented (Zeyde et al., 2012) with the use of Orthogonal Matching Pursuit (OMP) (Cai & Wang, 2011) as a lightweight alternative to the costly sparse decomposition assumed in this chapter, the cost of applying OMP for each patch still renders sparse coding unusable for some practical scenarios. In the following chapters we review different approaches that alleviate the high computational cost of sparse coding.

CHAPTER 6

Anchored Regression

As we have observed, both neighbor embedding and sparse coding introduce a high computational load that might be unacceptable for some applications in real-world scenarios. Fortunately, recent advances in learning-based super resolution have been presented, which allows for learning a certain mapping function from the manifold of the low-resolution patches (or features thereof) to that of high-resolution patches, following the manifold assumption already used in neighbor embedding (Chang et al., 2004). The mapping function between manifolds is assumed to be locally linear. Therefore, several linear regression functions are learned from the training examples and anchored to the manifold as a piecewise linearization.

In this chapter we first review the general framework for anchored regression and then we explore some extensions toward better quality and improved runtime that further push the usability of anchored regression to a broader set of applications.

6.1 ANCHORED REGRESSION FRAMEWORK

In this section we first review the problem statement common to many example-based approaches and direct it to the anchored regression framework first described by Timofte et al. (2013). Even though in this chapter we focus on external learning approaches, principles similar to those in anchor regression can also be efficiently combined with cross-scale self-similarity priors, as shown by J. Yang et al. (2013).

6.1.1 Problem Statement

Super resolution aims to upscale images with an unsatisfactory pixel resolution while preserving the visual sharpness and minimizing the back-projection error:

$$X = f(Y \uparrow s) \quad \text{s.t.} \quad X \downarrow s = Y, \tag{6.1}$$

where Y is the input image and X is the output upscaled image. The upsampling and downsampling operators (with their corresponding interpolation filters) are succinctly denoted by $\uparrow s$ and $\downarrow s$, respectively, and f is an arbitrarily complex function able to extend the spectrum of $Y \uparrow s$ to match the visual sharpness of the input image Y. The problem is usually addressed at a patch level, denoted with lower case, for example, y, x for input and output patches, respectively.

The external-learning super-resolution approach that we have reviewed so far, that is, sparse coding, tackles the problem by finding meaningful examples from which a high-resolution counterpart is already known, namely the couple of dictionaries D_l and D_h:

$$\min_{\beta} \|y - D_l\beta\|_2^2 + \lambda_p \|\beta\|_p, \tag{6.2}$$

where β selects and weighs the elements in the dictionary and λ_p weighs an L_p-norm regularization term, where typically $p = 1$ to enforce sparsity. The L_p-norm selection and the dictionary-building process depend on the chosen priors and can be used to further define the algorithm.

6.1.2 Anchored Neighbors

The work by Timofte et al. (2013) is remarkable for its low-complexity, while achieving competitive quality compared to neighbor embedding (NE) or sparse coding (SC) approaches. The method builds on a relaxation of the L_1-norm regularization commonly used in the mentioned counterparts, reformulating the problem as a least squares (LS) L_2-norm regularized regression, also known as Ridge Regression. While solving L_1-norm constrained minimization problems is computationally demanding (it does not admit a closed-form solution), relaxing it to a L_2-norm enables closed-form solutions. The new minimization problem reads

$$\min_{\beta} \|y_F - N_l\beta\|_2^2 + \lambda_2 \|\beta\|_2, \tag{6.3}$$

where N_l is the low-resolution neighborhood chosen to solve the problem (low-resolution atoms with nonzero weights) and y_F is a feature vector extracted from a low-resolution patch. The algebraic solution is

$$\beta = (N_l^T N_l + \lambda I)^{-1} N_l^T y_F. \tag{6.4}$$

The coefficients of β are applied to the corresponding high-resolution neighborhood N_h to reconstruct the high-resolution patch, that is, $x = N_h\beta$. This can also be written as the matrix multiplication $x = Ry_F$, where the projection matrix (i.e., the linear regressor) is calculated as

$$R = N_h(N_l^T N_l + \lambda_2 I)^{-1} N_l^T \qquad (6.5)$$

and can be computed offline, therefore removing the costly optimization problem during the inference stage.

Using sparse dictionaries with κ atoms, which can be trained, for example, with the K-SVD algorithm by Aharon et al. (2006), a linear regressor R_j can be anchored to each atom d_j in D_l, and the neighborhood N_l in Eq. (6.5) is selected from a k-Nearest Neighbor (k-NN) subset of D_l:

$$N_{l_j} = \text{kNN}(d_j, D_l). \qquad (6.6)$$

The SR problem can be addressed by finding the NN atom d_j of every input patch feature y_{iF} and applying the associated R_j to it. In the specific case of a neighborhood size $k = d_s$, only one general regressor is obtained whose neighborhood comprises all the atoms of the dictionary and consequently, does not require a NN search. This case is referred into the original paper as Global Regression (GR).

6.1.3 Inference by Linear Regression

Once the closest anchor point is found and exploiting the assumption of locally smooth mapping, linear regression can be applied to emphasize certain input features with the goal of recovering specific textures and structures for similar patches. The linear regression framework can be formulated as

$$x = \tilde{x} + R y_F, \qquad (6.7)$$

where $\tilde{x}$ is a coarse approximation of the high-resolution patch x. The choice of the method to obtain $\tilde{x}$ involves choosing a prior on how to approximate x. In the work of J. Yang et al. (2013) the in-place priors chosen as this initial approximation and Timofte et al. (2013) and Schulter et al. (2015) use bicubic interpolation assuming a smooth prior. The linear regression functions are trained to improve the reconstruction whenever the coarse prior is not sufficient.

Features

Intuitively, it makes sense to reduce the intrinsic dimensionality of the input data once a coarse approximation $\tilde{x}$ is available. One option is to choose a feature representation y_F with an explicitly smaller dimensionality than that of x or $\tilde{x}$. Supporting this, J. Yang et al. (2013) uses as an input feature the subtraction of the low-pass filtered in-place example to a patch in the upscaled image obtained by bicubic interpolation, thus introducing errors of the in-place prior in the low-frequency band into the model. Consequently, Timofte et al. (2013) and Schulter et al. (2015) use gradient-based features representing the high-frequency components that constitute the central problem in example-based super-resolution, because such information cannot be reconstructed by interpolation.

6.2 EXTENSIONS

This section discusses two complementary improvements for super resolution based on anchored regression. The first part addresses a nonintuitive shortcoming of the training scheme based on anchors described above and the second one tackles the dictionary size problem in the inference or testing stage by introducing faster search schemes.

6.2.1 Improved Accuracy

In super resolution by anchored regression, the objective of the supervised learning task leading to the linear regression functions $\{R_i\}$ is to obtain a locally accurate mapping function from low-resolution patches (or features) to high-resolution patches (or corrections to a coarse approximation thereof). For the sake of readability, the rest of the text will refer to high-resolution patches instead of their correction.

From a more general perspective, low-resolution feature vectors are assumed to form an input manifold M of dimension m, and high-resolution patches an equivalent target manifold N of dimension n. Formally, for training pairs (y_{Fi}, x_i) with $y_F \in M$ and $x_i \in N$, we wish to infer a mapping $\Psi : M \subseteq \mathbb{R}^m \to N \subseteq \mathbb{R}^n$.

As we have previously seen, the use of linear regression functions in anchored regression is influenced by the fact that they can be easily computed in closed form and applied as a matrix multiplication during the inference or testing stage. However, the overall mapping Ψ is highly complex and nonlinear (Peyré, 2009). To model the nonlinearity nature of the mapping, an ensemble of regressors $\{R_i\}$ is trained, representing a locally linear approximation of Ψ, under the assumption that both manifolds M and N have a similar local geometry. We can analyze the effect on the distribution of those regressors over the manifold (i.e., the anchor points) and the importance of properly choosing the N_l in Eq. (6.5), which shall intuitively lead to the improved training approach.

An overcomplete sparse representation can be obtained from the initial low-resolution training patches (or feature vectors) using, for example, K-SVD (Aharon et al., 2006). This compact dictionary D_l is used in the baseline anchored regression method described above, both as anchor points to the manifold and as data points for supervised learning (after pairing them with their high-resolution D_h counterparts). In an extreme setup with a single anchor point (Timofte et al., 2013), a unique regressor R_G is trained with all elements of the dictionary, thus accepting higher reconstruction errors due to the single linearization of the manifold.

Naturally, for a finer reconstruction, it is necessary to sample the underlying manifold more densely. Thus, more generally, anchored regression can directly use the dictionary points $\{D_1, \ldots, D_{d_s}\}$ as anchor points $\{A_1, \ldots, A_{d_s}\}$ and then build for each one of these atoms a neighborhood of k-NN within the same sparse dictionary D_l, following similar principles to those in sparse coding.

As we have seen in the previous chapter, performing a sparse decomposition of a high number of training patches efficiently compresses these data into a much smaller dictionary, yielding atoms which are ideally representative of the whole training dataset, that is, the whole manifold. This is the rationale behind their use as anchor points, but their nature renders them also suboptimal for neighborhood embedding. The reason is the necessary local condition for the linearity assumption, which is likely to be violated by neighborhoods spread over a large area of the underlying manifold. Indeed, due to the minimum-L_1-norm reconstruction constraint imposed in sparse dictionaries, atoms in the dictionary are not close in the Euclidean space, as shown in Fig. 6.1A.

This observation naturally leads to a better suited approach for training linear regressors for SR, which has been visited by C.-Y. Yang and Yang (2013), Pérez-Pellitero et al. (2014), and Timofte et al. (2014), among others. We can keep using sparse representations as anchor points to the manifold, but we can improve the locality of the neighborhoods by using raw training samples (i.e., feature vectors or patches). Fig. 6.1A shows how, by doing so, closer nearest neighbors can be found which, in turn, better fulfill the local condition.

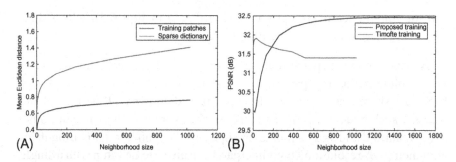

Fig. 6.1 (A) Mean Euclidean distance between atoms and their atom-neighborhoods for different neighborhood sizes. (B) PSNR (dB) for a reconstruction using anchored regression. 1024 anchor points were used to generate both charts. The improved training (dark curve) clearly outperforms the baseline approach.

Additionally, a higher number of local independent measurements is available (e.g., mean distance for 1000 neighbors in the raw-patch approach is comparable to a 40-atom neighborhood in the baseline or sparse approach) and we can control the number of k-NN selected, that is, it is not upper-bounded by the dictionary size. A low-dimensional toy example of the benefits of this alternative training scheme is shown in Fig. 6.2. Note that the availability of a higher number of training samples per anchor directly improves the condition of the supervised learning stage leading to the locally linear regression functions.

Fig. 6.1B shows the comparison between a baseline anchored regression (Timofte et al., 2013) and the improved training scheme in terms of PSNR of the reconstructed image. Both experiments use the same training dataset, and, for the dense neighbor embedding, the same l_2-normalized raw features used as input for the sparse dictionary optimization via K-SVD are also employed. Applying the improved training scheme allows anchored regression to achieve substantial quantitative quality improvements, which also translates into visual improvements.

6.2.2 Improved Runtime

When aiming at a fine modeling of the mapping function between low-resolution and high-resolution manifolds, an ideally large number of linear regressors should be trained to better represent the nonlinear function. Although other approaches for regression-based super resolution have also improved runtime with regard to other baselines, for example, Zeyde et al. (2012) vs. J. Yang et al. (2010) for sparse coding, finding the right anchor (or regression function) for each patch consumes most of the time in the

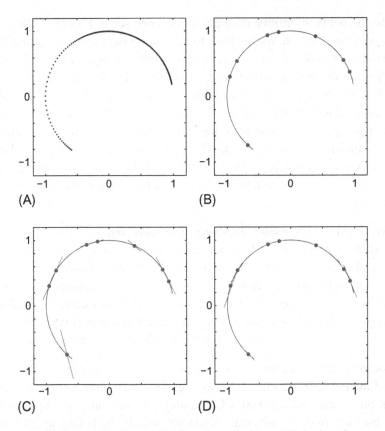

Fig. 6.2 A normalized toy manifold illustrating the effectiveness of the dense neighborhood sampling compared to sparse sampling. (A) Bidimensional manifold samples. (B) The manifold (line) and the sparse representation obtained with the K-SVD algorithm (dots) for just 8 atoms. (C) Local linear regressors (lines crossing the dots) trained with small neighborhoods ($k = 1$ neighbors for each anchor) obtained within the sparse dictionary (baseline approach stemming from sparse coding). (D) Linear regressors (almost perfectly tangent lines) obtained using the improved training with neighborhoods obtained within all manifold samples ($k = 10$).

anchored regression. For example, in Timofte et al. (2013, 2014), most of the encoding time, that is, the runtime after subtracting coarse estimation via bicubic interpolation and patch and feature extractions, is spent on this task, that is, ~96% of the time.

In order to improve the search efficiency in problems involving queries, search structures of sublinear complexity are often built, usually in the form of binary splits, for example, trees or hashing schemes (Breiman, 2001; Heo et al., 2012; Indyk & Motwani, 1998; J. Wang, Kumar, & Chang, 2010). Focusing on anchored regression, one might consider determining the search partitions directly with the set of anchor points, because those are the elements to retrieve during the inference stage. However, the small cardinality of this set would lead to an imprecise partitioning due to a shortage of sampling density. It is thus better to optimize the hashing function on the raw input samples, as depicted by the right-hand side of Fig. 6.3. By doing so, we can obtain a dense sampling (i.e., all training patches) during the optimization of the hashing functions, which results in meaningful partitions. The resulting search scheme, during the inference stage, consists of finding the k-ANN (Approximate Nearest Neighbor) anchors for every patch, as shown by the left-hand side of Fig. 6.3, and then selecting the most suitable of the related linear regression functions by re-ranking.

We could also consider tree-based methods, but we should note that an advantage of hashing schemes is that they provide low memory usage. Indeed, the number of splitting functions in hashing-based structures is $O(\log_2(n)$, whereas in tree-based structures $O(n)$ functions need to be stored, where n represents the number of clusters). In any case, it should also be noted that the storage cost of the partitioning schemes is typically much smaller than that required for storing the locally linear regression matrices.

Focusing on binary hashing techniques, these techniques aim to embed high-dimensional points into binary codes, thus providing a compact representation of high-dimensional data. Among their vast range of applications, they can be used for efficient similarity search, including approximate nearest-neighbor retrieval, because hashing codes preserve relative distances. There has recently been active research in data-dependent hashing functions opposed to hashing methods such as Indyk and Motwani (1998) which are data-independent. Data-dependent methods intend to better fit

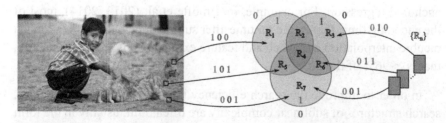

Fig. 6.3 Spherical hashing applied for fast anchored-regression super resolution problem. Spherical hashing functions are offline optimized on feature patch statistics creating a set of intersections of hyperspheres that translate into a hash code. In training time, the linear regression functions for the K-SVD anchor points are used to populate these intersections (or bins) and in testing time the hashing function is applied to each patch, which will directly map it to a regressor.

the hashing function to the data distribution (J. Wang et al., 2010; Weiss, Torralba, & Fergus, 2008) through an offline training stage.

Among other data-dependent methods, we can choose the Spherical Hashing algorithm by Heo et al. (2012), which has the advantage of being able to define closed regions in $\mathbb{R}^m$ with as few as one splitting function. This hashing framework is useful to model a fast search scheme and enables us to benefit from substantial speedups by reducing the NN search into applying a precomputed function, which conveniently scales with parallel implementations, as shown in Fig. 6.4.

Spherical hashing differs from other hashing approaches by setting hyperspheres to define hashing functions on behalf of the commonly used hyperplanes. A given hashing function $H(y_F) = (h_1(y_F), \ldots, h_c(y_F))$ maps points from $\mathbb{R}^m$ to a base 2 $\mathbb{N}^c$, that is, $\{0, 1\}^c$. Every hashing function $h_k(y_F)$ indicates whether the point y_F is inside kth hypersphere, modeled for this purpose as a *pivot* $p_k \in \mathbb{R}^m$ and a distance threshold (i.e., radius of the hypersphere) $t_k \in \mathbb{R}^+$ as:

$$h_k(y_F) = \begin{cases} 0 & \text{when } d(p_k, y_F) > t_k \\ 1 & \text{when } d(d_k, y_F) \leq t_k \end{cases}, \tag{6.8}$$

where $d(p_k, y_F)$ denotes a distance metric (e.g., Euclidean distance) between two points in $\mathbb{R}^m$. The advantages of using hyperspheres instead of hyperplanes is the ability to define closed tighter subspaces in $\mathbb{R}^m$ as intersection of hyperspheres. An iterative optimization training process is proposed in Heo et al. (2012) to obtain the set $\{p_k, t_k\}$, aiming a balanced partitioning of the training data and independence between hashing functions.

As discussed above, it is better to perform the iterative hashing-function optimization onto the complete set of input patch feature vectors from

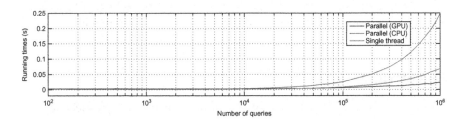

Fig. 6.4 Running times measured when computing 6-bit hash codes (6 hyperspheres in spherical hashing) for increasing number of queries (in logarithmic axis and without re-ranking) for single-threaded (CPU) and parallel (CPU and GPU) implementations.

training images, so that $H(y_F)$ adapts to the natural image distribution in the feature space. The spherical hashing search scheme becomes symmetrical, as shown in Fig. 6.3, that is, both image and anchor points have to be labeled with binary codes. This can be intuitively understood as creating NN subspace groups (we refer to them by *bins*), which we label with a certain number of anchors and related regression functions by applying the same hashing functions to the anchor points. Relating a hash code with a subset of regression functions can be done during training time.

The inference search approach returns k-NN for each input patch, thus not ensuring that all input image patches have a related regressor, that is, whenever the patch is not within the k-NN of any of the anchor points. Two solutions can be adopted:

(a) Use a general regressor for patches which fall in a cluster without any anchor point.
(b) Use the regressor of the closest labeled hash code calculated with the spherical Hamming distance.

The spherical Hamming distance is defined as

$$d_{SH}(a,b) = \frac{\sum(a \oplus b)}{\sum(a \wedge b)}, \tag{6.9}$$

where $\oplus$ is the XOR bit-wise operation and $\wedge$ is the AND bit-wise operation (Heo et al., 2012). Note that despite the lack of guarantees, it rarely happens that a patch is not within any of the k-NN regressors (e.g., for a reasonable parameter of 6 hyperspheres and 1024 centroids it never occurs). Because significant differences in performance will not appear in most cases, we can select option (a) as the lowest complexity solution.

Because two or more anchors and their related regression functions can be assigned to a single bin, it is common in the literature to perform a re-ranking strategy (He & Sun, 2012), which results in a small linear minimum-distance search over a reduced set of anchors for each input patch.

6.3 PERFORMANCE

In order to quantify the impact of the improvements with respect to the baseline anchored regression and other techniques described in the previous chapters, we compare their performance in terms of reconstruction accuracy and runtime. In order to understand the limits and improvements for different inputs, we can perform extensive experiments with image resolutions ranging from 2.5k pixels to 2M pixels, thus showing the performance for classic literature testing images and also demonstrating how these algorithms perform in realistic upscaling scenarios. Thus, we can base this on the benchmark by Timofte et al. (2013) and further extend it, for example, by adding two more datasets to the well-known *Set5* or *Set14*. The 24 image *kodak* dataset that we have also seen in the performance assessment of other models is also included in the comparison, as well as a more realistic *2k* dataset, which is an image set of nine sharp images obtained from the internet with a pixel resolution of 1920×1080.

All the experiments are run on an Intel-based workstation, and most of the codes and suitable parameters are directly available in the website of Timofte et al. (2013), including the global regressor (GR) and an implementation of the baseline anchored regression stemming from sparse coding. The rest of compared methods are the sparse coding super-resolution of Zeyde et al. (2012), an implementation of the Neighbor-Embedding regression with least squares (NE-LS), and the method by Chang et al. (2004) (NE+LLE), and the NonNegative Least Squares (NE+NNLS) method of Bevilacqua et al. (2012).

6.3.1 Implementation Details

Whereas the rest of the methods in the comparison are entirely implemented in MATLAB, the hashing-based improved anchored regression can greatly benefit from using OpenCL (even if running on the same CPU) for the most time-consuming stages, that is, the computation of the hash functions, the reranking stage to determine the best regression function (or nearest-neighbor respective anchor point), and the final product of the selected regression matrix and feature vector leading to the regressed correction for each patch. All methods use the same sparse dictionary of 1024 atoms obtained through K-SVD.

Coarse Approximation

As discussed above, a reasonable selection for the coarse approximation $\tilde{x}$ is bicubic interpolation. In contrast with cross-scale self-similarity approaches like J. Yang et al. (2013), using an interpolation-based approximation does not limit the upscaling steps for super-resolution. Note that in-place examples are only meaningful for very small magnification factors, which further limit their applicability with fast applications in mind.

Feature Vectors

The feature vector for each patch y_F can be composed of the features used by Zeyde et al. (2012), Timofte et al. (2013), and Pérez-Pellitero et al. (2014), among others. These features consist in the first and second order derivative filters responses for all pixels in the patch compressed via Principal Components Analysis (PCA) and truncating the coefficients, such that the feature vector conserves 99.9% of its energy. The use of this type of feature typically results in an enhanced accuracy, thanks to the underlying exploitation of image information beyond the spatial limits of the patch induced by the spatial extents of the derivative filters.

Supervised Learning

We can also use the L_2-norm regularized linear regressor described by Eq. (6.3), following the regression function scheme proposed by Timofte et al. (2013, 2014) and Pérez-Pellitero et al. (2014), among others. The advantage of introducing the regularization term is the enhanced numerical stability leading to better generalization, even in cases where few example pairs are available.

Hashing

A suitable configuration is a 6-bit spherical hashing (6 hyperspheres) for 1024 anchors, which can be increased by one unit every time we double the number of anchors. The selection of the number of hyperspheres responds to a trade-off between quality and speed because, when we decrease the number of hyperspheres, we have more collisions of regressors (i.e., more than one regressor arrives to the same bin) which, thanks to the re-ranking process, can lead to a more exact nearest-neighbor search. This behavior can be observed in Fig. 6.5. A reasonable choice for the size of the neighborhood used to estimate the hashing parameters (centroids and thresholds) is in the order of 1000 k-NN.

6.3.2 Benchmarking

Table 6.1 shows objective performance measurements in terms of PSNR (dB) and execution time (s). For both measures, the improved anchored regression algorithm is the best performing through all the tested datasets.

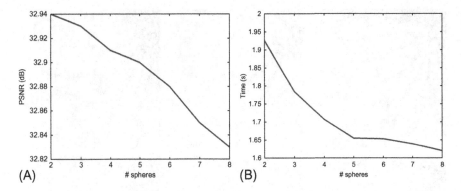

Fig. 6.5 *Effect of the number of hyperspheres for fast anchored regression in terms of (A) PSNR and (B) time. Note the presence of a speed vs. quality trade-off.*

Quality

The improvement in PSNR is more noticeable for smaller magnification factors, that is, $3\times$, where improvements of up to 0.3 dB can be achieved when compared to the baseline anchored regression. This result quantifies the gain due to the improved training strategy presented above. An interesting point to discuss about this quality improvement is that the additional memory used for storing the locally linear regression functions in the baseline anchored regression is not optimally exploited, because the achieved quality is just comparable to that of well-engineered sparse coding approaches like Zeyde et al. (2012). Thanks to the better exploitation of the training information in the improved training approach, the additional memory cost spent on storing the regression coefficients also returns enhancements in terms of quality.

Fig. 6.6 provides sample results for a visual qualitative assessment. The improved anchored regression method obtains more natural-looking and sharper edges, and also allows us to strongly reduce ringing when compared to the other approaches. A representative example supporting this observation is the *butterfly* image.

Computational Cost

In terms of running time, the hash-based improved anchored regression has consistent speed-ups in all datasets and all upscaling factors. When compared to GR (which is the fastest of the compared methods, because it does not require the NN anchor search at the expense of an important

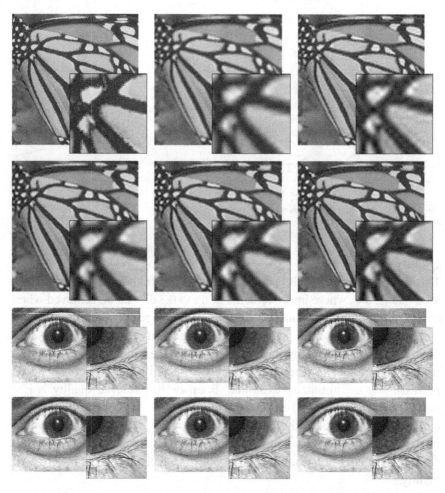

Fig. 6.6 *Visual qualitative assessment of* 3× *upscaling for images from datasets Set5 and 2k. From left to right and top to bottom: Original (groundtruth), bicubic interpolation, Global Regressor (Timofte et al., 2013), Sparse Coding (Zeyde et al., 2012), baseline anchored regression (Timofte et al., 2013), and improved anchored regression (Pérez-Pellitero et al., 2014).*

gap in reconstruction quality), the speed-ups are ranging from 2× to 3×, essentially coming from the introduction of OpenCL in the pipeline (which can be achieved even without emphasis on performance). The speed-ups with respect to the baseline anchored regression range from 3× to 4× and, for the rest of the compared methods, the running times are several orders of magnitudes slower, because they do not benefit from the relaxation introduced by anchored regression.

Table 6.1 Performance of 3× and 4× Magnification in Terms of Averaged PSNR (dB) and Averaged Execution Time (s) on the Typical Set14; and Kodak Datasets, and on a 1920 × 1080 (2k) Dataset (Best Results in Bold)

	MF	Bicubic		Sparse		GR		Anchored		NE+LS		NE+NNLS		NE+LLE		Improved	
		PSNR	Time	PSNR	Time	PSNR	Time	PSNR	Time	PSNR	Time	PSNR	Time	PSNR	Time	PSNR	Time
Set14	3	27.54	0.002	28.67	2.981	28.31	0.528	28.65	0.771	28.59	2.854	28.44	25.372	28.60	4.356	**28.93**	**0.188**
	4	26.00	0.003	26.88	1.862	26.60	0.458	26.85	0.584	26.81	1.716	26.72	14.146	26.81	2.623	**27.04**	**0.184**
Kodak	3	28.43	0.003	29.22	5.126	28.98	0.921	29.21	1.335	29.17	4.829	29.04	44.102	29.17	7.353	**29.42**	**0.314**
	4	27.23	0.003	27.83	3.194	27.64	0.757	27.80	1.022	27.77	3.003	27.71	24.428	27.77	4.678	**27.92**	**0.309**
2k	3	31.73	0.007	32.63	27.622	32.45	4.860	32.68	7.123	32.62	26.194	32.51	242.875	32.65	40.389	**32.88**	**1.652**
	4	30.28	0.006	30.97	17.225	30.81	3.968	30.99	5.344	30.94	16.363	30.87	136.058	30.96	25.967	**31.04**	**1.578**

6.4 DISCUSSION

In this chapter we have presented the anchored regression framework and have extended it in two directions: an improved training stage toward higher accuracy and an efficient hashing-based approach toward reduced running time during the inference or testing stage. These improvements allow us to build on the already excellent performance of a baseline anchored regression approach. The main advantages of anchored regression are, on the one hand, that the running time can be greatly reduced, thanks to the relaxation of the sparsity constraint in sparse coding and, on the other hand, that the additional memory used to store the locally linear regression functions can embed additional information from the training dataset that leads to noticeable quality improvements. The further introduction of hashing allows us to scale the method to an arbitrarily large number of anchor points without overly affecting the running time, thus we can aim at obtaining both quality improvements from the optimized training stage, and also substantial speedups from hashing schemes like the spherical hashing described above and used for determining the best regression function for each patch.

The combination of unsupervised learning of anchor points or centroids via dictionary learning approaches like K-SVD (Aharon et al., 2006) and fast local mapping function selection via hashing during runtime results in better quality (for most natural images) and reduced runtime than that obtained by the techniques described in previous chapters, including both cross-scale self-similarity approaches and the $L1$-constrained sparse coding. Building on these results, in the next chapter we review a powerful unified framework for both unsupervised learning and efficient inference that results in dramatic speedups and enhanced quality.

CHAPTER 7

Trees and Forests

This chapter discusses a further refinement in example-based super resolution with external learning that provides a fast, scalable, and accurate
solution by tackling the most demanding problem in the inference stage
(i.e., the selection of the local linearization of the mapping function for
each patch) and the corresponding training process, especially targeting
the unsupervised part of the training (i.e., clustering). Because hierarchical
approaches based on regression trees are capable of solving both the
clustering and efficient inference subproblems, in the following we explore
their applicability with the goal of a fast and accurate super-resolution
framework for external (offline) learning. The rest of the chapter provides
in depth coverage of

(a) Hierarchical manifold learning, including an improved strategy with
bimodal trees that allows grouping *antipodal* patches and provides fast
local linearization search.
(b) An efficient Local Naive Bayes strategy for per-patch tree selection
during the inference or testing stage, providing the advantages of forests
with a reduced computational cost slightly higher than that of using a
single tree in terms of running time.
(c) A super-resolution method, namely *Naive Bayes Super-Resolution Forest* (NBSRF) that amply improves speed and also objective and perceived quality, and is suitable for real-time applications with reasonable
computational power.

Even though the use of regression trees and forests is well-known (Breiman,
2001; Criminisi et al., 2011) and their direct application to super resolution
with external learning can be considered with excellent expected results
(J.-J. Huang, Siu, & Liu, 2015; Schulter et al., 2015), this chapter focuses
on two key observations that lead to further speed and quality improvements
with respect to the known framework.

In essence, the improved forest framework is strongly related to C.-
Y. Yang and Yang (2013), in the sense that it also aims at providing a direct

mapping from coarse to high-resolution patches by dividing the input coarse space into clusters and then learning a locally linear mapping function to high resolution, and also to Timofte et al. (2014) and Pérez-Pellitero et al. (2014), so that the mapping function actually produces a correction layer for an initial coarse estimation of the high-resolution patches.

7.1 HIERARCHICAL MANIFOLD LEARNING

The general overview of the hierarchical manifold learning stage, whose output is a partition tree, is shown in Fig. 7.1. The coarse (upscaled) estimate of X can be obtained via iterative back-projection (IBP) (Irani & Peleg, 1990; J. Yang et al., 2010) from the low-resolution input image Y

$$\tilde{X}^{(n+1)} := \tilde{X}^{(n)} + H_u * ((Y - (\tilde{X}^{(n)} * H_d) \downarrow s) \uparrow s), \qquad (7.1)$$

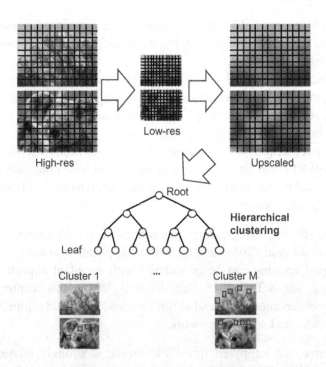

Fig. 7.1 Overview of the training stages involved in hierarchical clustering. The example input images are downscaled and upscaled by the desired upscaling factor; once the upscaled images are divided into overlapping patches, the latter are recursively divided into different clusters by minimizing a certain metric regarding the intra-class variance in each subcluster.

where the superscript (n) indicates the iteration, H_d is a downsampling filter avoiding the presence of aliasing in the back-projected image and H_u is an interpolation filter, which can be the same one used for bicubic interpolation. Typically, a small number of iterations, for example, 2 or 3, is sufficient to reach convergence and provide a better coarse estimate than that obtained with bicubic interpolation, including a higher presence of texture at the expense of a certain degree of ringing around edges that can be corrected through the regression scheme.

At a patch level, the reconstruction model continues as

$$x = \tilde{x} + \mathcal{R}(\tilde{x} - \bar{x}) = \tilde{x} + \mathcal{R}(\tilde{x}_0), \tag{7.2}$$

where $\mathcal{R}$ is a nonlinear regression function and $\tilde{x}_0$ is the mean-subtracted (or floating) version of $\tilde{x}$. Whereas other approaches use handcrafted features as input to the regression problem (e.g., Pérez-Pellitero et al., 2014; Timofte et al., 2013, 2014; Zeyde et al., 2012) or the external learning frameworks described in former chapters, below we shall see how features can be adaptively computed while traversing the tree in order to select one of the M available local linearizations R_i of $\mathcal{R}$ obtained via supervised learning.

Contrast Normalization

We can further observe that given a patch x with a certain structure, the scaled version αx contains the same structure just with different contrast. Because this argument is valid for both the high-resolution patch x and the coarse approximation $\tilde{x}_0$ when they are related by a linear transform, it makes sense to group all patches with the same structure by normalizing them:

$$\hat{x} = \frac{1}{\|\tilde{x}_0\|_2}\tilde{x}_0. \tag{7.3}$$

The result is that all possible patch structures lie on a unitary hypersphere centered at the origin akin to the toy example in Fig. 7.3 top. This observation, combined with the zero-mean or floating patch, actually further reduces the span of the manifold, as shown in Fig. 7.2. Because the higher-dimensional space corresponding to actual image patches cannot be properly visualized, in the following, the projection of a sphere will be used to represent the actual intersection of a hypersphere and a hyperplane resulting from the combination of the mean subtraction and patch normalization operations.

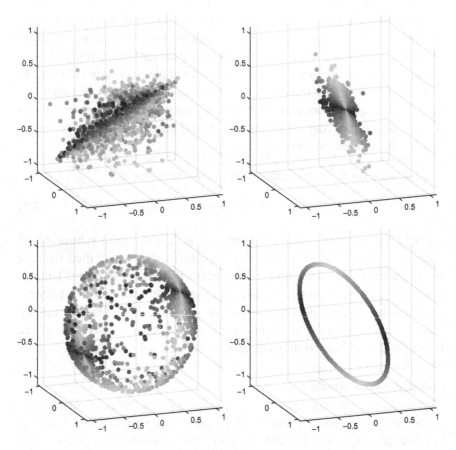

Fig. 7.2 *From left to right and top to bottom: distribution of three-dimensional (column) patches; distribution after mean subtraction (hyperplane); distribution after normalization (hypersphere), and after the combination of both (intersection).*

Unimodal Trees

Based on the good results in J. Yang et al. (2013) for in-place example regression, one might consider a similar space partitioning strategy, that is, using unimodal partition trees: for each node, proceed to split data based on the thresholding of a feature (i.e., the response to a certain filter). This is the mechanism underlying the PCA tree (McNames, 2001), its random projection approximation (Freund et al., 2007) and also the faster k-D trees used in Schulter et al. (2015). In the latter, a set of features is precomputed for all data and the splitting is based on the thresholding of the most sensitive feature for each node, whereas the PCA tree and its approximation provide an adaptive (and naturally costlier) computation of relevant features during the root-to-leaf tree traversal.

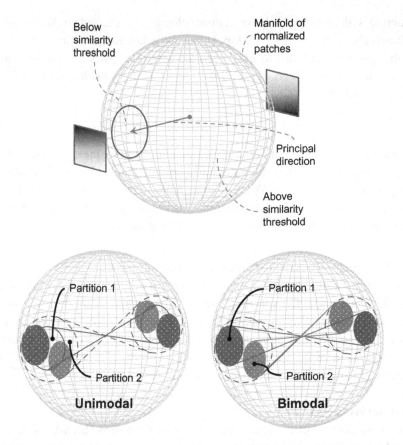

Fig. 7.3 Top, typical unimodal partitions on a normalized-feature space. The spherical cap (delimited by the solid line) is the fraction of the manifold that can be described with a single principal direction. Bottom, clustering for antipodal patch grouping with unimodal and bimodal partitions. Note the more balanced partitions of the shaded data clusters possible with the bimodal scheme.

The strategy of projection and thresholding in unimodal trees is valid when data are distributed as a thin manifold (Freund et al., 2007). However, inspecting the configuration of the problem, depicted in Fig. 7.3 top (with all data lying on the intersection between a hypersphere and a hyperplane), we can intuit that partitioning data in this fashion would be rather suboptimal. Indeed, the partition resulting from unimodal approaches is rather unbalanced with normalized patches: the subset of data lying out of the inclusion partition (projection above threshold) is much more heterogeneous than the one lying inside (below threshold).

7.1.1 Antipodal Symmetry

In addition to the normalization of data, it is also important to observe that antipodal points, that is, $\hat{x}$ and $-\hat{x}$, are also representations of the same structure with a scaling factor or contrast change. An example of such pair of points is also shown in Fig. 7.3 top. Hence, an efficient hierarchical partition of the space should aim to also keep all antipodal pairs within the same cluster. In order to do so, the optimal metric is the Absolute Value of the Cosine Similarity (AVCS)

$$\text{AVCS}(\hat{a}, \hat{b}) = |\hat{a} \cdot \hat{b}|, \tag{7.4}$$

where $\hat{a}$ and $\hat{b}$ are two data on the unitary hypersphere, that is, normalized. Fig. 7.3 bottom illustrates the potentially better balanced bimodal partitions when combined with the AVCS metric. Note that the unimodal partitions may yield a rather compact centered cluster and a surrounding one with high variance vs. the more uniform bimodal partitions.

7.1.2 Bimodal Regression Tree Training

During the offline training stage, the partition tree can be built such that, for each node, the splitting criterion is to discriminate the two most relevant clusters grouping antipodal data. Given the AVCS metric, using linear strategies to discriminate clusters, for example, PCA, is not suitable (resulting in the unbalanced partitions shown in Fig. 7.3, bottom left). We therefore need to rely on subspace clustering techniques.

Unsupervised Learning

For simplicity and efficiency, a modification of k-means (Lloyd, 1982) can be adopted. The modification, which can be interpreted as an antipodally invariant spherical k-means algorithm. Even with Forgy (random) initialization, which leads to randomized trees when more than a single instance is learned, this choice provides PSNR performance similar to the much costlier K-SVD (Aharon et al., 2006) used for dictionary training in sparse coding and anchored regression. The modifications of the two iterative stages of the algorithm for k classes C_i, $1 \le i \le k$ result in the iteration

1. **E-step.** $C_i^{(n)} = \{\hat{x} : |\hat{x} \cdot \mu_i^{(n)}| \ge |\hat{x} \cdot \mu_j^{(n)}| \forall j, 1 \le j \le k\}.$
2. **M-step.** $\mu_i^{(n+1)} = \| \sum_{\hat{x} \in C_i^{(n)}} \sigma \hat{x} \|_2^{-1} \sum_{\hat{x} \in C_i^{(n)}} \sigma \hat{x},$

where $\sigma = \text{sign}(\hat{x} \cdot \mu_i^{(n)})$. The resulting partition criterion for a node in the *bimodal* tree is $\arg\max_i |\mu_i \cdot \hat{x}|$, $i = 1, 2$. Note that this is fundamentally different from the criteria found in unimodal trees, where only one projection takes place. In Section 7.3 we discuss the advantages of using the bimodal tree for space partitioning.

Supervised Learning

Because during training we have access to coarse estimates of patches and their actual high-resolution counterparts (low-resolution images are generated by downscaling the set of training images as shown in Fig. 7.1), all $\{\tilde{x}_0\}$, $\{\tilde{x}\}$, and $\{x\}$ corresponding to all $\{\hat{x}\}$ lying in one of the M clusters (tree leaves) are used to compute the local linearization of $\mathcal{R}$ in the form of the regression matrix $R_i, 1 \leq i \leq M$. Let $\tilde{\mathbf{X}}_0$, $\tilde{\mathbf{X}}$ and $\mathbf{X}$ be the matrices obtained by stacking all these (vectorized) patches as columns. The expression to compute each regression matrix can be derived from Eq. (7.2) as

$$R_i = (1 + \lambda)(\mathbf{X} - \tilde{\mathbf{X}})\tilde{\mathbf{X}}_0^\top (\tilde{\mathbf{X}}_0\tilde{\mathbf{X}}_0^\top + \lambda\mathbf{I})^{-1}, \qquad (7.5)$$

where λ is a small regularization factor, e.g., 10^{-4}, to avoid numerical stability issues.

7.2 NAIVE BAYES SUPER-RESOLUTION FOREST

Tree ensembles are well-known for many vision applications (Breiman, 2001; Criminisi et al., 2011), and have also been employed for super-resolution based on learning stages similar to the ones described above (J. B. Huang et al., 2015; Schulter et al., 2015). As an extension to these approaches, we can exploit a tree selection strategy inspired by Bernard, Heutte, and Adam (2009). The rationale is that combining all trees in the ensemble might not always be the best possible option:

- On the one hand, performing a large number of linear regressions for each datum might become prohibitively costly when the number of trees in the ensemble is large.
- On the other, as shown in Bernard et al. (2009) for classification tasks, combining a large number of tree decisions does not necessarily produce better results, because some trees could be deteriorating the ensemble performance (e.g., observe the results for 16 trees with the more typical *average* scheme using all available trees and the efficient NBSRF using only one in Table 7.2).

For efficiency reasons, we should aim at a scheme where a reduced number of trees (in an extreme case just a single tree) is selected from the entire ensemble. As we shall see in Section 7.3, this simple strategy, which we shall succinctly name Naive Bayes Super-Resolution Forest (NBSRF), can provide an excellent quality vs. running time trade-off. Fig. 7.4 illustrates

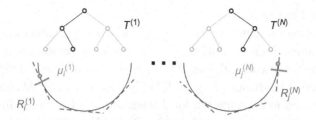

Fig. 7.4 *The main problem solved by NBSRF. Given a regression-tree ensemble, select the tree $T^{(k)}$ providing the best local linearization of the mapping function for the given datum.*

the advantage of using an ensemble of trees in this manner. If we are able to quantify the selectivity of each tree $T^{(k)}, 1 \leq k \leq N$ with respect to an input datum ($\hat{x}$, green dot on the sampled manifolds represented by the semi-circumferences in the figure), we can perform a much more accurate regression than that attainable by considering a random single tree. A naive solution to this problem would be to choose that tree for which the AVCS of the datum and the corresponding leaf mode is maximum. However, this criterion would discard the precious information about the space partition that leads to the leaf node in each tree and provide suboptimal performance, as reflected by the results of the *leaf*-based selection experiment in Table 7.2.

7.2.1 Data Distribution

In first place, we need to model the data distribution in each node to be able to quantify the selectivity of the tree with respect to each datum. The Von Mises-Fisher distribution (Fisher, 1953), which models distributions over a unit hypersphere, is defined as

$$f(x; \mu, \kappa) = C(\kappa) \exp\left(\kappa(\mu \cdot x)\right), \qquad (7.6)$$

where μ is a mean direction, κ is a concentration parameter that determines the dispersion from the central mode and $C(\kappa)$ is a normalizing constant. Because our clusters are designed to contain antipodal data by exploiting the AVCS metric, the Von Mises-Fisher distribution must be correspondingly adapted:

$$f'(x; \mu, \kappa) = C'(\kappa) \exp\left(\kappa|\mu \cdot x|\right), \qquad (7.7)$$

where $C'(\kappa)$ normalizes the modified distribution. We note that, for each node in the tree, the underlying data distribution is actually seen as a mixture of two *antipodal* Von Mises-Fisher distributions. For simplicity, in the following we shall assume that both components in the mixture have the same concentration κ, which empirically validates as a reasonable assumption.

7.2.2 Local Naive Bayes Selection

In order to establish the criterion to choose the most selective tree $T^{(k*)}$ for a given patch $\hat{x}$, we can rely on the Local Naive Bayes framework already used for adaptive sparse coding in Chapter 5 and introduced by McCann and Lowe (2012) after conveniently adapting it to the data distribution in the bimodal tree ensemble setup.

Based on the original Naive Bayes derivation (Boiman et al., 2008), if we assume a noninformative prior over regressors across all trees, each patch $\hat{x}$ is most accurately mapped by a regressor $R_i^{(k*)}$ from tree $T^{(k*)}$ following

$$R_i^{(k*)} = \arg\max_{R_i^{(k)}} p(R_i^{(k)}|\hat{x}) = \arg\max_{R_i^{(k)}} \log p(\hat{x}|R_i^{(k)}). \qquad (7.8)$$

If each tree has M leaf nodes (and therefore regressors), a total number of $L = log_2(M)$ node responses or features $f_l^{(k)}$ are computed from patch $\hat{x}$ in each root-to-leaf tree traversal. The Naive Bayes assumption of feature independence results in

$$R_i^{(k*)} = \arg\max_{R_i^{(k)}} \sum_{l=1}^{L} \log p(f_l^{(k)}|R_i^{(k)}), \quad 1 \le k \le N. \qquad (7.9)$$

The problem with this formulation is that it requires computing the likelihoods for all possible paths across the tree. Fortunately, the alternative formulation by McCann and Lowe (2012) allows us to progress. The effect of each node response to a patch $\hat{x}$ can be expressed as a log-odds update. This is extremely useful for trees, because it allows us to restrict updates to only those nodes for which the descriptor gives significant evidence (i.e., the visited nodes along the root-to-leaf traversal). Let $R_i^{(k)}$ be some linear mapping and $\bar{R}_i^{(k)}$ the set of all other linear mappings. The odds $\mathcal{O}$ for the mapping $R_i^{(k)}$ with uniform priors is given by

$$\mathcal{O}(R_i^{(k)}) = \frac{p(R_i^{(k)}|\hat{x})}{p(\bar{R}_i^{(k)}|\hat{x})} = \prod_{l=1}^{L} \frac{p(f_l^{(k)}|R_i^{(k)})}{p(f_l^{(k)}|\bar{R}_i^{(k)})}. \qquad (7.10)$$

The alternative classification rule expressed in terms of log-odds increments is

$$R_i^{(k*)} = \arg\max_{R_i^{(k)}} \sum_{l=1}^{L} \log \frac{p(f_l^{(k)}|R_i^{(k)})}{p(f_l^{(k)}|\bar{R}_i^{(k)})}, \quad 1 \le k \le N. \qquad (7.11)$$

In the Local Naive Bayes formulation, $p(f_l^{(k)}|\bar{R}_i^{(k)})$ can be approximated by the likelihood of the alternative (or discarded) partition in each traversed node. The resulting method, using the antipodal Von Mises-Fisher distribution mixture and the bimodal antipodally invariant tree forest, is described in Algorithm 3. Note that, because we assume that the concentrations κ are the same for both clusters in each node, the local term in the sum of Eq. (7.11) reduces to $|\mu_1 \cdot \hat{x}| - |\mu_2 \cdot \hat{x}|$, where μ_1 is the most suitable mode. In the pseudocode, the node selection during the root-to-leaf traversal is implicit and $R[\mu_L^{(k*)}]$ represents the regression matrix of the chosen leaf's mode in the optimal tree.

Algorithm 3 Naive Bayes SR Forest

Data: Patch $\hat{x}$, forest $\{\mu_{i,l}^{(k)}\}$, regressors $R[\mu_L^{(k)}]$

for *each tree $k \leq N$* **do**

    $lodd^{(k)} \leftarrow 0$

    for *each level $0 \leq l < L$* **do**

        if $|\hat{x} \cdot \mu_{1,l}^{(k)}| \geq |\hat{x} \cdot \mu_{2,l}^{(k)}|$ **then**

            $lodd^{(k)} \leftarrow lodd^{(k)} + |\mu_{1,l}^{(k)} \cdot \hat{x}| - |\mu_{2,l}^{(k)} \cdot \hat{x}|$

        else

            $lodd^{(k)} \leftarrow lodd^{(k)} + |\mu_{2,l}^{(k)} \cdot \hat{x}| - |\mu_{1,l}^{(k)} \cdot \hat{x}|$

return $k* \leftarrow \arg\max_k lodd^{(k)}$ and $R[\mu_L^{(k*)}]$

7.3 PERFORMANCE

In order to assess the performance of NBSRF, we can choose a selection of some of the best performing super-resolution methods, including

- The sparse coding method based on K-SVD dictionaries by Zeyde et al. (2012) (referred to as *Sparse coding*).
- The baseline anchored regression by Timofte et al. (2013) (*Anchored*).
- The convolutional network approach by Dong et al. (2014) (*CNN*).
- The training-improved anchored regression by Timofte et al. (2014) (*A+*).
- The *Forest* with 15 trees of $L = 16$ layers by Schulter et al. (2015) using the alternative training for better PSNR.

All the codes can be obtained from the respective authors' websites. For CNN, the public implementation is slower than the one used in their original paper, so the runtime is not meaningful. All methods use the training dataset of 91 images from J. Yang et al. (2010) and, unless otherwise stated, the default configurations provided by their authors, including the 12 exponentially decaying scales of the training images in A+ and ASRF. For augmenting the training data, NBSRF has used 16 linearly decaying scales with a slope of -0.25.

7.3.1 Implementation

The main performance gain of NBSRF comes from the algorithmic choice of using a hierarchical clustering strategy, which results in a logarithmic search cost in comparison to the exhaustive search common in most other methods. Whereas the bottleneck of this fast approach lies on the linear regression, this is also kept to a minimum by the Naive Bayes tree selection approach (only one regression has to be computed). The structure of the proposed method makes it a suitable candidate for parallelized implementation, for example, using OpenMP or OpenCL. The described method can also be extended by applying feature extraction and PCA compression of the input as in Zeyde et al. (2012), Timofte et al. (2013, 2014), and Pérez-Pellitero et al. (2014), which shall result in smaller linear regression matrices and thus further reduced computational cost.

Algorithm 4 Heuristic Tree Selection

Data: Patch $\hat{x}$, forest $\{\mu_{i,l}^{(k)}\}$, regressors $R[\mu_L^{(k)}]$

for *each tree $k \leq N$* **do**

   $prob^{(k)} \leftarrow 1$

   for *each level $0 \leq l < L$* **do**

      if $|\hat{x} \cdot \mu_{1,l}^{(k)}| \geq |\hat{x} \cdot \mu_{2,l}^{(k)}|$ **then**

          $prob^{(k)} \leftarrow prob^{(k)}(|\mu_{1,l}^{(k)} \cdot \hat{x}| - |\mu_{2,l}^{(k)} \cdot \hat{x}|)$

      else

          $prob^{(k)} \leftarrow prob^{(k)}(|\mu_{2,l}^{(k)} \cdot \hat{x}| - |\mu_{1,l}^{(k)} \cdot \hat{x}|)$

return $k* \leftarrow \arg\max_k prob^{(k)}$ and $R[\mu_L^{(k*)}]$

A further heuristic modification is shown in Algorithm 4. In this case, the difference between the responses to the two features in each mode is interpreted as the probability that the node provides a good partition for the datum. Assuming independence between nodes, the probability for each tree can be modeled as the product of the probabilities of all traversed nodes. A slight computational advantage comes from the fact that, when one tree is very unlikely, that is, both modes in a node are equally suitable for a datum, we may be able to terminate the tree traversal at an early stage. Because the bottleneck resides on the matrix-vector product, this gain is marginal, but, in some scenarios, this alternative tree selection scheme might produce better results. Other criteria for selecting a (group of) suitable tree(s) might be devised, but this falls beyond the scope of this book.

Parameters

A suitable configuration for NBSRF can start with a low-resolution patch size of 3×3 pixels, which produces progressively larger coarse inputs with the upscaling factor s, for example, 6×6 for $s = 2$, and so on. The number of trees N can be set to a value around 8 and the number of tree layers L is 11, which translates into $M = 2048$ regressors per tree. Whereas this configuration is not necessarily optimal for all applications, it suffices to produce excellent performance. Despite the large scale of the parameters to be learned, the training is relatively fast, ranging from around 20 minutes for the $4\times$ upscaling model to around one hour for the $2\times$ model on a typical Intel-based workstation. It should be noted that the training time would clearly be the bottleneck in applications with nonnegligible unknown blur, where the effect of blur must be taken into account when generating the models.

Benchmark

All methods, including NBSRF, have been tested on the same workstation. We can use the common benchmark in recent super-resolution publications (Dong et al., 2014; Pérez-Pellitero et al., 2014; Salvador & Pérez-Pellitero, 2015; Timofte et al., 2013, 2014), consisting of $2\times$, $3\times$, and $4\times$ upscaling tasks for two sets of 5 (*Set5*) and 14 (*Set14*) images of different but relatively low resolutions, which can be extended, for example, with the *Kodak* dataset. The latter provides 24 images free of compression artifacts with larger resolution, hence slightly closer to a real-world scenario. Table 7.1 shows the average PSNR (dB), Information Fidelity Criterion (IFC) (Sheikh, Bovik, & de Veciana, 2005; C.-Y. Yang, Ma, & Yang, 2014) and runtimes obtained by each method in all scenarios. The Information Fidelity criterion is relevant for the super-resolution problem, as shown by

C.-Y. Yang et al. (2014). We note that NBSRF is by far the fastest (up to one order of magnitude with respect to the runner-up improved anchored regression or A+ in 2× upscaling) thanks to the fast clustering and inference strategy. NBSRF is especially better than other alternatives for images with a large degree of sharp edges, where the locality of the examples used to train the regression matrices is more critical. Fig. 7.6 provides a qualitative comparison on the upscaling results of the best performing super-resolution methods for some of the images in the three datasets. In general, we can appreciate an enhanced robustness of NBSRF to ringing and aliasing artifacts.

7.3.2 Analysis and Scalability

The baseline configuration of $N = 8$ trees and $M = 2048$ leaves per tree suffices to showcase the excellent performance in comparison to alternative approaches. However, it may be interesting to test with different parameters in order to understand the scalability of the method. The response, in terms of running time and reconstruction quality (PSNR), to variations to the most relevant parameters, is shown in Fig. 7.5.

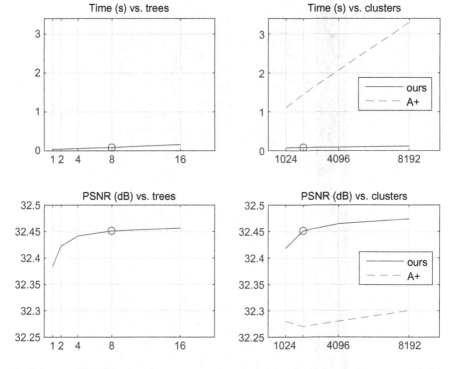

Fig. 7.5 Average PSNR (dB) and time (s) vs. varying numbers of trees (left) and leaf nodes—or clusters—per tree (right) for 2× upscaling on Set14. The baseline configuration is marked by the small circle.

Table 7.1 Average PSNR (dB), Information Fidelity Criterion and Running Time (s) on Set5, Set14 and Kodak for 2×, 3×, and 4× Scaling (Best Results in Bold)

	s	Bicubic			Sparse Coding			Anchored			CNN			Forest			A+			NBSRF		
		PSNR	IFC	Time	PSNR	IFC	Time	PSNR	IFC	Time	PSNR	IFC	Time	PSNR	IFC	Time	PSNR	IFC	Time	PSNR	IFC	Time
Set5	2	33.66	5.859	0.002	35.78	7.479	1.992	35.83	7.658	0.495	36.34	7.268	3.205	36.69	8.075	0.817	36.55	7.994	0.514	**36.76**	**8.257**	**0.036**
	3	30.39	3.509	0.002	31.90	4.372	0.934	31.92	4.473	0.340	32.39	4.257	3.364	32.57	4.772	0.624	32.59	4.779	0.328	**32.75**	**4.882**	**0.053**
	4	28.42	2.302	0.001	29.69	2.889	0.559	29.69	2.951	0.227	30.09	2.822	3.106	30.20	3.131	0.705	30.28	3.186	0.225	**30.44**	**3.241**	**0.055**
Set14	2	30.23	5.898	0.002	31.81	7.329	4.015	31.80	7.445	1.101	32.18	7.053	6.515	32.36	7.780	1.427	32.28	7.736	1.105	**32.45**	**7.941**	**0.061**
	3	27.54	3.402	0.002	28.67	4.102	1.881	28.65	4.173	0.65	29.00	3.978	6.414	29.12	4.384	1.112	29.13	4.392	0.662	**29.25**	**4.484**	**0.080**
	4	26.00	2.211	0.002	26.88	2.672	1.147	26.85	2.725	0.469	27.20	2.592	6.382	27.31	2.854	0.910	27.32	2.895	0.468	**27.42**	**2.931**	**0.086**
Kodak	2	30.85	5.457	0.002	32.19	6.625	7.015	32.24	6.743	1.886	32.63	6.451	10.993	32.76	6.938	2.293	32.71	6.928	1.984	**32.81**	**7.222**	**0.105**
	3	28.43	3.116	0.002	29.22	3.679	3.300	29.21	3.740	1.139	29.43	3.658	11.065	29.53	3.859	1.728	29.57	3.889	1.154	**29.63**	**4.026**	**0.138**
	4	27.23	1.984	0.002	27.83	2.361	2.012	27.80	2.393	0.817	27.94	2.288	11.102	28.06	2.454	1.469	28.10	2.514	0.810	**28.17**	**2.590**	**0.153**

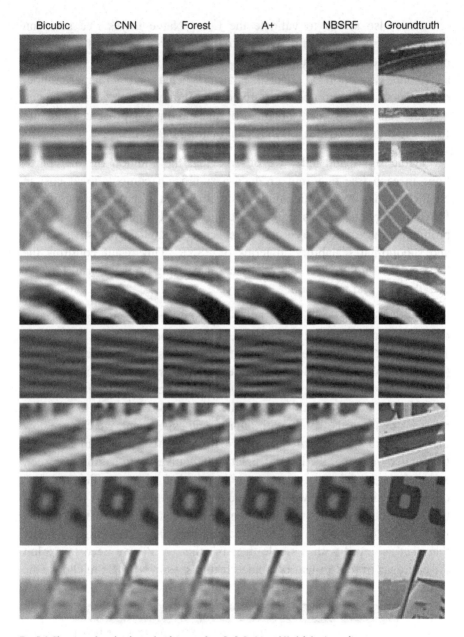

Fig. 7.6 Close-ups of results obtained with images from Set5, Set14, and Kodak for 4× scaling.

The left-hand side shows the runtime and PSNR evolution of NBSRF with different numbers of trees. We can observe that the computational cost of adding trees is linear, but with a small slope, because regardless of the number of trees, only one regression operation takes place. The bottom left chart also serves to validate the Local Naive Bayes tree selection algorithm. The addition of more trees to the ensemble consistently produces better accuracy, even though just one of them is actually used to infer the appearance correction for the coarse patch. Whereas an even larger number of trees does not seem necessary given the saturation of the curve, we can note the fair improvement obtained by the multitree approach: Switching from 1 to 8 trees provides a PSNR gain of around 0.07 dB.

On the right-hand side, we observe that the addition of finer partitions in each tree does not produce a significant computational cost in NBSRF thanks to the hierarchical structure, yet it provides significant PSNR performance gains. In contrast, the overall runner-up A+ shows a prohibitive increase of the computational cost (due to the exhaustive search) and suboptimal scalability in terms of PSNR. This result confirms the value of the bimodal tree with antipodal clustering as a powerful tool for classification and regression.

Table 7.2 shows in more detail the effect of the different design decisions on $2\times$ upscaling on Set14 for increasing numbers of trees with $L = 11$ layers ($M = 2048$ leaves). The first columns of the baseline Forest (Schulter et al., 2015) and NBSRF essentially show the improvement of the bimodal clustering strategy. In the *bicubic* experiment, NBSRF is initialized with bicubic interpolation, instead of Iterative Back-Projection to show the relative impact of the latter. With the *random* experiment, we can see how the Local Naive Bayes criterion of NBSRF is clearly better than a random tree choice (note that the latter is practically equivalent to having one tree), and with the *leaf* experiment, we can observe that it is not sufficient to just observe the similarity between data and leaf modes to determine the optimal tree, as pointed out above. Note that, when discarding the information from the higher levels in the tree, the performance is only slightly better than that achieved with a single tree. In other words, we need to exploit the entire set of root-to-leaf computed features, as in NBSRF, to choose the

Table 7.2 PSNR (dB) for 2× Scaling With $L = 11$ on Set14

	1 Tree	2 Trees	4 Trees	8 Trees	16 Trees
Forest (Schulter et al., 2015)	32.11	32.16	32.21	32.21	32.22
bicubic	32.28	32.32	32.34	32.35	32.35
random	32.38	32.39	32.40	32.39	32.39
leaf	32.38	32.40	32.40	32.41	32.40
average	32.38	32.43	32.45	32.46	32.45
NBSRF	32.38	32.42	32.44	32.45	32.46

optimal tree. Finally, the *average* experiment shows that carrying out all the regressions and averaging (classical random forest) provides, in practice, the same accuracy, yet it is much costlier because the linear regression has to be computed for all trees in the ensemble. The last column of the comparison in Table 7.2 shows that tree selection can even outperform averaging in some cases where a considerable number of trees are suboptimal for a large amount of patches.

7.4 DISCUSSION

In this chapter we have reviewed in depth a state-of-the-art forest-based super-resolution method aiming to high performance in both quality and running time. NBSRF builds on a new interpretation of the coarse-patch space, where antipodal normalized patches (i.e., pairs of patches with the same structure but different sign) are actually considered to be part of the same clique. This observation is consequently exploited by a hierarchical manifold learning strategy based on a partition tree with bimodal nodes, where antipodal patches are effectively clustered together and both children subnodes have comparable homogeneity, thus leading to an overall better space sampling.

We have also seen how, in order to further extend the accuracy of the local linearizations of the coarse-to-fine mapping, the use of tree ensembles can be efficiently employed through the selection of the optimal regression tree, which can be based on a Local Naive Bayes criterion or other alternatives. Overall, the methods described in this chapter provide the best running time vs. quality trade-off, but this comes at the expense of a high memory load to store the regression parameters of a relatively large number of local linearizations.

Some open questions common to the external learning methods presented so far are

- How can we obtain a competitive running time and quality with a relatively low memory usage? Or, in other words: How can we design compact models providing excellent performance?
- What is the optimal representation of the input data (i.e., features) to provide optimal reconstruction quality?

Both questions are answered with the alternative family of deep learning methods reviewed in the next chapter.

CHAPTER 8

Deep Learning

In recent years, advances in deep learning have revolutionized the applicability of machine learning in a large number of problems. Naturally, all computer vision problems can be reinterpreted as shallower or deeper networks designed to represent different levels of abstractions of the training data. The advantage of deep learning with respect to the rest of machine learning methods is that practically all aspects of the model are directly learned from the data, starting with the lowest-level features presenting a suitable representation of the data and progressively providing higher-level abstractions for each specific problem as we advance through the different network layers. An overview of the general deep learning problem applied to Super Resolution is shown in Fig. 8.1.

In this chapter we first present a short review on deep learning with focus on convolutional networks and then proceed with some useful types of networks and a discussion of their advantages.

8.1 NEURAL NETWORKS

It is well known that many computer vision and image processing algorithms offer drastically different performances based on the chosen feature representation of the input data. We have already seen part of this problem in previous chapters. In some cases, using gradient-based features might provide better performance than just considering raw pixels.

The motivation of deep learning can be found in the debate between representation (or feature) engineering vs. learning. In the former, features are manually defined, which implies:

- Reliance on human domain knowledge more than on the available data.
- Design is independent from the system's training.
- Difficult tuning when the number of parameters in the system is large.

Example-Based Super Resolution. http://dx.doi.org/10.1016/B978-0-12-809703-8.00008-3

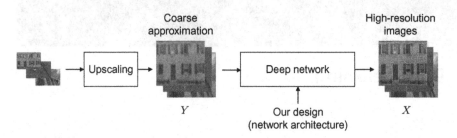

Fig. 8.1 *In deep learning, the super-resolution problem translates into a specification of a network architecture. All parameters in the model are automatically learned from training data, starting from the low-level representation or features of the input image, and ending with the reconstruction stage producing the output image.*

In contrast, learned representations or features provide some clear advantages:

- Joint learning of feature transformations and system parameters.
- Large number of parameters are automatically handled.
- It makes better usage of massive data collections (i.e., big data).

Thus, deep learning can be seen as the learning of hierarchical feature representations. Most interestingly, each hierarchy level is able to disentangle multiple factors that might appear coupled in the data, for example, in a face capture identity, pose, expression, or age are some of the factors that appear combined.

An interesting fact about deep learning is that the design is inspired by biological systems. For example, it has been shown that human brains also process visual information through a multilayer structure: the visual cortex (Krüger et al., 2013). The deep learning framework, which also benefits from large-scale computers (clusters, Graphics Processor Units, upcoming neural chips), is able to solve general learning problems, which strongly contrasts with former machine learning models that are task-specific and present a loose tie with biological systems.

Learning to Learn

The biological inspiration of neural networks was already present before 1986, with multilayer perceptrons. A small multilayer perceptron is illustrated in Fig. 8.2, where the operation that takes place in each neuron is also shown. The most common early choice for the nonlinear function f used to be a sigmoid function by resemblance with the electrical response

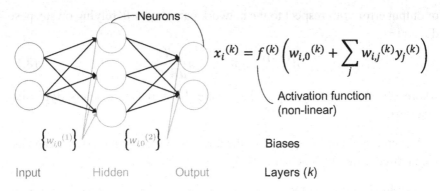

$$x_i^{(k)} = f^{(k)}\left(w_{i,0}^{(k)} + \sum_j w_{i,j}^{(k)} y_j^{(k)}\right)$$

Activation function
(non-linear)

Biases

Input   Hidden   Output   Layers (k)

Fig. 8.2 A small multilayer perceptron composed by an input layer, a single hidden layer and an output layer. Each neuron combines the outputs of the former layer's neurons and a bias value and produces a nonlinear output. Typically, full-connectivity is chosen in this type of network.

of biological neurons. The training was carried out by means of perceptron convergence, which did not provide a useful hierarchical feature extraction.

This problem was overcome by the work of Rumelhart et al. (1988), with the introduction of the still used back-propagation algorithm for network training, illustrated in Fig. 8.3 for a multilayer perceptron. The advantages are that the internal or hidden layers are actually capable of representing features of the task domain, that regularities in the task are captured by their interactions and, most importantly, that for the first time a solution is provided to general learning problems. The goal is to minimize the loss l

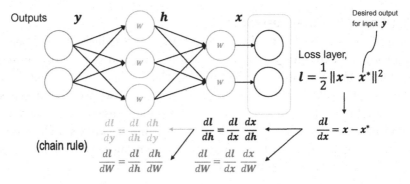

Fig. 8.3 The back-propagation algorithm attempts to minimize the output error by computing the derivative of the error at the output and back-propagating it layer by layer by means of the derivative chain rule. The goal is to estimate the optimal parameters W such that a specific loss l is minimized following a steepest descent criterion.

or output error with respect to the network parameters W relying on steepest descent:

$$W^{(n+1)} := W^{(n)} - \eta \frac{dl}{dW^{(n)}}, \qquad (8.1)$$

where η is the learning step and $W^{(0)}$ are the initial parameters (typically random).

Depending on the frequency of the updates to the parameters, we can talk about three different types of training:

- **Online training.** Network parameters are updated after processing each example.
- **Mini-batch training.** The entire set of examples is divided into small mini-batches. Network parameters are updated after accumulating the errors of all examples in the mini-batch.
- **Batch training.** Similar to mini-batch training, but processing all available examples before applying updates.

The event of processing all available training examples is commonly called an *epoch*. In general, training will evolve more speedily with online training and more robustly with batch training. In general, mini-batch training is chosen as a good balance between both. It is also convenient to name each type of processing direction during training:

- **Forward pass.** Regular network's processing direction (i.e., set of computations that produce the output from the input).
- **Backward pass.** Back-propagation direction (i.e., computations to produce derivative of input error with respect to output error and parameters).

8.1.1 Convolutional networks

The main idea behind convolutional networks is to reduce the number of parameters by exploiting the properties of locality and stationarity present in natural images, as illustrated in Fig. 8.4. The origins can be found in the work by LeCun et al. (1989), where convolutional networks are introduced as a powerful mechanism to improve generalization through the imposition of constraints known from the task domain to the network's architecture. The resulting reduction of free parameters translates into an increased probability of correct generalization.

Another advantage of convolutional networks is that they accept inputs of different sizes, in contrast with fully connected networks where the

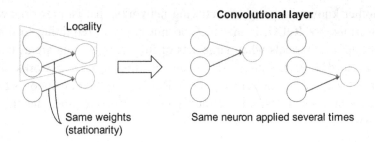

Fig. 8.4 Convolutional networks exploit locality and stationarity to reduce the number of parameters to estimate.

number of inputs and outputs is fixed by the network architecture. This property is especially useful for image enhancement applications like Super Resolution.

Improving Learning

Deep autoencoders are networks able to compress and decompress the input images, that is, the output is an approximation of the input reconstructed by the network after reducing the dimensionality in internal layers. Hinton and Salkhutdinov (2006) and Bengio, Lamblin, Popovici, and Larochelle (2007) show how this type of network benefits from a layer-wise pretraining. The use of pretraining is shown to produce internal high-level abstractions of the input and results in effective training for arbitrarily deep networks. In more detail, each pair of consecutive layers can be isolated and pretrained with the goal of determining the interactions between consecutive layers. Then, the subnets can be stacked and trained with back-propagation to fine-tune them for much better performance.

Another way to improve learning is through the use of rectifying nonlinearities at the output of neurons instead of earlier sigmoid ones. The rectifying nonlinearity, commonly called rectifying linear unit (ReLU), can be formulated as

$$ReLU(y) = \max(y, 0). \tag{8.2}$$

Targeting vision applications, Nair and Hinton (2010) show how results are improved for both object recognition and face verification. The advantage of rectifying nonlinearities is that the output is invariant to intensity, whereas sigmoid nonlinearities produce a range compression that, in turn, reduces the separability of data.

Another known property of rectifying networks, that is, networks were nonlinearities are ReLU, is that they do not require pretraining to obtain close-to-optimal models when large sets of fully labeled data are available (Glorot, Bordes, & Bengio, 2011). The resulting sparse networks show sparsity (derived from the zero-regime in ReLU) and their behavior is close to that in biological neurons in the main operating regime, that is, the linear part.

More recently, network parameters regularization via *dropout* has shown to reduce overfitting and thus learn more robust features. Dropout is based on the base back-propagation algorithm and extends it by randomly disabling neurons during the backward pass with a certain probability. The final network weights are normalized by dividing by the dropout probability. In the Imagenet challenge, the introduction of large networks with dropout by Krizhevsky, Sutskever, and Hinton (2012) allowed the reduction of the classification error from 26.2% (runner up) to 15.3%.

Architecture Trade-offs

Networks can be designed, ranging from thin and shallow to fat and deep. Usually, network design follows a thin and deep or fat and shallow design. The former considers a large number of layers (deep) with a constrained number of neurons and extents of the local interactions (thin), whereas the latter presents a large number of neurons per layer and large extents for local interactions (fat) with a small amount of layers (shallow). The possible designs are illustrated in Fig. 8.5. The advantage of deep networks is a higher capability to model nonlinear functions, whereas that of fat networks is more robustness against overfitting. A good balance between

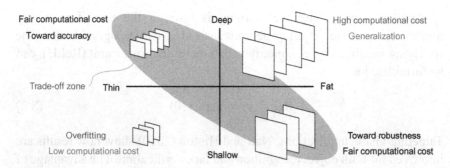

Fig. 8.5 *The design of a neural network's architecture responds to a trade-off involving accuracy, generalization, and computational cost. Practical designs usually lie in the trade-off region.*

accuracy, generalization, and computational cost will ultimately determine the network architecture.

8.1.2 Applications

Neural networks present desirable properties for most machine learning applications, including early vision and image enhancement such as denoising, deblurring, or Super Resolution. One of the first contemporary papers on denoising (Jain & Seung, 2008) adopts convolutional networks with sigmoids. Most interestingly, deep networks are even able to perform well in blind denoising scenarios, where the noise variance is unknown, but still automatically handled by a 6-layer network trained with images corrupted with different noise levels.

Another possibility for denoising is to use multilayer perceptrons (Burger, Schuler, & Harmeling, 2012). Being more generic than convolutional networks, the performance is close to that of well-engineered state-of-the-art denoising methods, such as BM3D (Dabov, Foi, Katkovnik, & Egiazarian, 2007), with the advantage of being easy to generalize to many different types of noise. For that purpose, the only necessary action is to modify the training data to be corrupted by the noise type to be removed.

In Schuler, Burger, Harmeling, and Schölkopf (2013), multilayer perceptrons have also been shown to outperform state-of-the-art methods for deblurring in the presence of noise (Dabov, Foi, Katkovnik, & Egiazarian, 2008) thanks to the compensation of artifacts introduced during the deconvolution process learned automatically during the network training. Besides, it can also be used to automatically handle different types of noise by conveniently modifying the training data. Other challenging tasks such as dirt and rain artifact removal can also be automated with convolutional networks (Eigen, Krishnan, & Fergus, 2013).

8.2 NETWORKS FOR SUPER RESOLUTION

We have observed how neural networks can be successfully applied for a wide variety of computer vision problems, so now it is the right time to overview their application for Super Resolution. Cui et al. (2014) present an iterative approach based on collaborative autoencoders, the goal of which is to provide high-resolution versions of the input patches that are *compatible* in the sense that the overlapping is constructive and keeps the reconstructed detail. This mechanism, which can be interpreted as a spatial regularization, is in practice, costly due to the iterative application with small upscaling steps, so in the following, we review more efficient approaches based on convolutional networks.

8.2.1 Conventional convolutional network

Following the diagram in Fig. 8.1, a feed-forward network can be built to regress high-resolution images from coarse initial approximations obtained, for example, by interpolation-based upscaling (Dong et al., 2014, 2016).

Even though deep learning provides automatic selection of suitable data representations, that is, features, domain knowledge can still be useful to decide the architecture of the network. Taking sparse coding for Super Resolution as a reference, we can regard the pipeline as a concatenation of three processing stages:

1. Feature vector extraction from input patches.
2. A nonlinear mapping composed of the sparse decomposition of input feature vectors with respect to a compact overcomplete dictionary and the reconstruction of high-resolution patches with respect to the corresponding high-resolution dictionary.
3. Image reconstruction by patch overlapping.

As we shall see, convolutional networks provide an approximation to this pipeline without explicitly instantiating the low-resolution and high-resolution dictionaries.

Specification
A convolutional network architecture can be described by means of a small number of metaparameters:

- Number of layers
- Type of nonlinear activation functions in each layer
- Number of neurons in each layer
- Extents of local interactions in each layer

These metaparameters, which in turn define the actual parameters or weights W in the network, can be represented as shown in Fig. 8.6. Each convolutional layer presents two sets of parameters: a bias vector (with one entry in the vector for each neuron), that is, assumed implicit in the graphical representation and a tensor where the dimensions correspond to the spatial

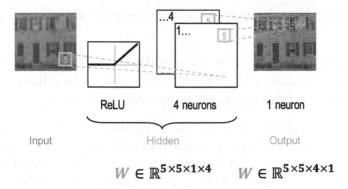

$$W \in \mathbb{R}^{5 \times 5 \times 1 \times 4} \qquad W \in \mathbb{R}^{5 \times 5 \times 4 \times 1}$$

Fig. 8.6 Graphical representation of a convolutional network architecture. In this case, a 2-layer network with a 4-neuron hidden layer with ReLU nonlinear activations, a 1-neuron output layer without nonlinear activation, and 5 × 5 spatial interactions are shown. An additional bias parameter for each neuron is implicitly assumed.

two-dimensional extents of the interactions, the number of input dimensions (i.e., the number of output dimensions or neurons in the precedent layer), and the number of output dimensions (i.e., the number of neurons in the current layer). Because the role of the input layer is to just fetch the input data, this layer is assumed implicit and not counted in the following.

Sparse Coding Approximation

Going back to our target problem, the three stages in sparse coding can be approximated by a shallow convolutional network with three layers. The architecture, presented by Dong et al. (2014), is shown in Fig. 8.7. In order to describe the network's behavior, it is useful to consider all ReLUs in the diagram as part of the intermediate layer and the first and third layers as

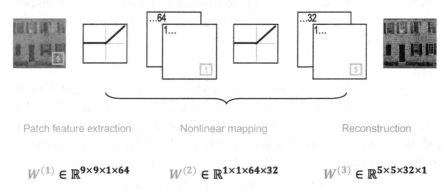

$$W^{(1)} \in \mathbb{R}^{9 \times 9 \times 1 \times 64} \qquad W^{(2)} \in \mathbb{R}^{1 \times 1 \times 64 \times 32} \qquad W^{(3)} \in \mathbb{R}^{5 \times 5 \times 32 \times 1}$$

Fig. 8.7 Graphical representation of a neural network inspired by the sparse coding pipeline (Dong et al., 2014).

purely linear. Note that the third layer (reconstruction) is actually purely linear.

This reordering enables the interpretation of the first layer as a dense 9×9 patch extraction stage (e.g., with sliding window or full overlapping, or a different *stride*) producing 64-dimensional linear features.

The second layer with the two ReLU operations and its 1×1 spatial extents provides a nonlinear mapping from 64-dimensional low-resolution features to 32-dimensional high-resolution ones. Note that, in contrast with regular sparse coding, the absence of explicit dictionaries translates into an output in terms of features, rather than reconstructed patches.

Thus, the third layer, which tackles the image reconstruction problem, provides a linear combination of the 32-dimensional high-resolution features with a weighted combination of the overlapping contributions of 5×5 patches.

Improved Mapping
The bottleneck of this approach lies in the computational capability of the nonlinear mapping. Because actual dictionaries are not available in the network, the accuracy can be greatly enhanced by considering interactions with wider spatial extents. In Dong et al. (2016) this idea is followed to propose an alternative (and naturally more computationally expensive) network with wider spatial extents, that is, 5×5 pixels in the intermediate layer.

8.2.2 Sparse coding network
A closer approximation to sparse coding can be accomplished by designing networks that explicitly model low-resolution and high-resolution dictionaries (Z. Wang et al., 2015) in a direct translation of fast sparse coding algorithms to the deep learning framework.

ISTA
An efficient solution for the sparse coding decomposition problem is provided by the Iterative Shrinkage and Thresholding Algorithm (ISTA) by Daubechies, Defrise, and DeMol (2004). Given the column input vector y and the column-wise low-resolution dictionary D_l, ISTA provides the sparse code e of y with respect to D_l through the recursion

$$e^{(0)} = 0 \quad e^{(n+1)} = h_\tau \left(D_l^\top y + S e^{(n)} \right), \qquad (8.3)$$

where the subscript (n) indicates the iteration, $S = LI - D_l^\top D_l$ is a mutual inhibition matrix, I an identity matrix, and L an upper bound of the largest eigenvalue of $D_l^\top D_l$. The nonlinear h_τ is an element-wise shrinking operator

$$h_\tau(z_i) = \text{sign}(z_i) \max (|z_i| - \tau_i, 0). \tag{8.4}$$

The graphical representation of this recursive algorithm is shown in Fig. 8.8.

LISTA

The unrolling of ISTA leads to the feed-forward scheme shown in Fig. 8.9. The Learned Iterative Shrinkage and Thresholding Algorithm (LISTA) presented by Gregor and LeCun (2010) provides sparse coding functionality for deep learning. The main advantage of LISTA with respect to ISTA is that all parameters, including the shrinkage thresholds, the mutual inhibition matrix, and even the overcomplete dictionary can be learned from data. In terms of extensions of generic convolutional networks, this scheme provides further constraints (beyond locality and stationarity) which result in enhanced learning efficiency and generalization.

The application to super resolution, presented by Z. Wang et al. (2015), has been shown to suffice with a single unrolled iteration of LISTA to provide excellent performance. The scheme, shown in Fig. 8.10, includes

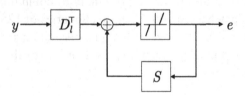

Fig. 8.8 The Iterative Shrinking and Thresholding Algorithm (ISTA) efficiently obtains the sparse decomposition e of y with respect to the overcomplete dictionary D_l. Adapted from Gregor, K., & LeCun, Y. (2010). Learning fast approximations of sparse coding. In Proceedings of the international conference on machine learning (p. 399–406).

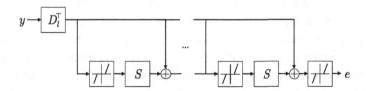

Fig. 8.9 Learned ISTA unfolds the recursion in ISTA and allows learning optimal parameters in deep learning. Adapted from Gregor, K., & LeCun, Y. (2010). Learning fast approximations of sparse coding. In Proceedings of the international conference on machine learning (p. 399–406).

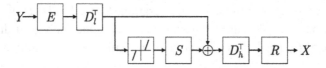

Fig. 8.10 *The application of LISTA for super resolution allows combining the power of learned end-to-end parameters from convolutional networks and domain knowledge about sparse coding.* Adapted from Wang, Z., Liu, D., Yang, J., Han, W., & Huang, T. (2015). Deep networks for image super-resolution with sparse prior. In Proceedings of IEEE international conference on computer vision (p. 370–378).

a patch and feature extraction convolutional layer E, a high-resolution dictionary D_h, and a reconstruction stage including patch overlapping R. Naturally, after learning all parameters through back-propagation, the design inspired by sparse coding does not necessarily lead to a sparse coding network, but it does allow for reduction of the number of required parameters and shortening the learning time, thanks to the exploitation of knowledge domain.

For example, thanks to the end-to-end parameter learning in convolutional networks, dictionaries can be much more compact than in traditional sparse coding and provide better performance in terms of visual quality and objective metrics. The input patch can be set to sizes around 9×9 pixels and the dimensionality of the feature representation, combining contributions from overlapping patches, to 100. Using dictionaries of 128 atoms, the size of D_l is thus 100×128. The size of the high-resolution patch can be set to sizes as low as 5×5 pixels, which implies an even smaller high-resolution dictionary D_h.

8.3 PERFORMANCE

Convolutional networks for super resolution can be trained by minimizing the squared error between the estimated output and the groundtruth images. Even though this metric does not strictly represent perceptual qualities about the reconstructed images, it allows for computing gradients smoothly and optimize PSNR measurements. As we shall see, the choice of the network architecture does have a strong impact in the perceived accuracy. In this section, we discuss some of the most relevant aspects in network training and then proceed with a benchmark for the two discussed alternatives.

8.3.1 Implementation

A large number of software packages are available for deep learning, including Caffe (C++), Theano (Python), MatConvNet (Matlab), or Tensor-Flow (Python), to name a few of the most commonly used ones. Whereas the inference stage with convolutional networks directly handles inputs of different sizes, for training it is necessary that all data have the same dimensions. This condition can be easily fulfilled by generating overlapping subimages of fixed size out of the original images. Thus, the training pipeline is such as:

1. Downscale the training images H by factor s and upscale the result by the same factor s to produce the coarse network input C.
2. Generate a set of fixed size overlapping images Y and X out of C and H, respectively.
3. Apply back-propagation with input Y and desired output X to generate the network's optimal parameters.

The inference stage consists of simply:

1. Upscale the input image Y_0 by the desired factor s to produce the coarse estimate Y.
2. Apply network onto Y to generate the estimate of the high-resolution version X.

Training Cost

One of the major shortcomings in deep learning is that the fine-tuning of all parameters in the network takes a considerably larger amount of time than classical machine learning. Despite of the reduction in number of parameters enabled by the adoption of convolutional networks instead of fully connected ones, training the conventional convolutional network described above can take in up to three days with relatively efficient implementations of the back-propagation algorithm. This is the time required to compute around 10^9 back-propagation steps with the relatively shallow network described above. In contrast, the sparse-coding network design allows for reduction of the number of back-propagations by almost two orders of magnitude, thus greatly simplifying the training.

Iterative Application

Even though one of the attractive points in external learning is the ability to upscale in a single step even for large magnifying factors, a noticeable quality improvement can be achieved for these large factors by iteratively applying a network trained for $s = 2\times$ upscaling, as for example, in Z. Wang et al. (2015). It is also possible to tune a second network to map the intermediate output from the initial $2\times$ network to the final desired resolution, thus taking into account the specific signal statistics of the intermediate stage when deciding the optimal network parameters. Naturally, both of these options will incur a higher computational load, but in scenarios constrained by quality, this is a simple modification to be taken into account.

8.3.2 Benchmark

Using the de-facto standard Set5, Set14, and BSD100 datasets introduced in previous chapters, the conventional convolutional network (CNN) and the sparse coding-inspired one (convolutional sparse-coding network or CSCN) can be numerically compared. In Table 8.1 we can see how the sparse coding network provides better accuracy despite the drastically reduced number of parameters and required training time. About the conventional network, we can see how the version with larger spatial extents (9-5-5) is largely superior to the faster but less computationally powerful 9-1-5 version. The sparse-coding network is in general the clear winner in the comparison. It is important to note that the implementation of CSCN for large upscaling factors is iterative, whereas the other networks proceed in a single step.

Table 8.1 PSNR (dB) and SSIM for Different Upscaling Factors on Set5, Set14, and BSD100 (Best Results in Bold)

Dataset	s	CNN 9-1-5		CNN 9-5-5		CSCN	
		PSNR	SSIM	PSNR	SSIM	PSNR	SSIM
Set5	2	36.33	0.951	36.67	0.953	**36.93**	**0.956**
	3	32.38	0.903	32.76	0.908	**33.09**	**0.915**
	4	30.08	0.854	30.48	0.863	**30.87**	**0.873**
Set14	2	32.18	0.904	32.44	**0.907**	**32.56**	**0.907**
	3	29.01	0.815	29.30	0.822	**29.40**	**0.824**
	4	27.21	0.741	27.49	0.751	**27.63**	**0.758**
BSD100	2	31.10	0.884	31.36	**0.888**	**31.41**	**0.888**
	3	28.21	0.779	28.41	0.786	**28.50**	**0.789**
	4	26.69	0.702	26.90	0.711	**27.03**	**0.716**

8.4 DISCUSSION

In this chapter we have reviewed the main principles behind the deep learning framework, especially focusing on the application of convolutional neural networks. This type of neural networks is suitable for a large variety of computer vision problems and, naturally, also for super resolution. When applied to super resolution, a conventional convolutional network automatically provides great performance at the cost of a long training stage involving the repeated application of the back-propagation learning algorithm in a high amount of passes over the training data. In contrast, a design exploiting domain knowledge on super resolution like the sparse-coding inspired convolutional network allows greatly reducing the number of free parameters in the network, thus simplifying the training stage and providing better generalization.

The main advantage of deep learning in comparison to the frameworks presented in the previous chapters is the power to determine hierarchical descriptions of the visual data that are directly learned from the data. This favorable condition of deep learning allows, among other, to automatically determine the optimal low-level features to represent our data for the specific upscaling problem. Despite being finely tuned for minimal squared error, we can observe that convolutional networks also provide good performance in terms of perceptual metrics more representative of the qualities observed and detected by the human visual system. This outcome, even if not conclusive, results from the biologically inspired design of convolutional networks, partly resembling the layered structure of the visual cortex.

With this chapter we close the technical description of the most successful approaches for example-based super resolution with external learning. In the next and last chapter, we review the state of the art as described throughout the different chapters into this book and introduce some of the current challenges and problems requiring the application of some form of super resolution.

CHAPTER *9*

Conclusions

Throughout the book we have covered the most successful algorithmic approaches for super resolution and, simultaneously, the working principles of the underlying machine learning models that have been proposed during the last years. In this chapter we briefly overview the most relevant aspects, advantages and shortcomings of the different models discussed in the former chapters and conclude with some perspectives about current challenges and possible future lines of work.

9.1 OVERVIEW

We have seen that classic super resolution, that is, multiframe or reconstruction-based super resolution, is constrained by numerical bounds that limit its applicability to scenarios where a only a small upscaling factor is required. This model, based on reversing the imaging process with multiple captured images, is mainly affected by imperfections in the registration step, and in smaller grade also in the other stages, that is, interpolation and restoration. Regardless of the number of available images, the effective resolution gain is bounded by a $1.6\times$ upscaling factor with realistic imaging conditions (Baker & Kanade, 2002; Z. Lin & Shum, 2004). With complex video contents showing fast motion in different directions, the robust applicability is very limited.

Consequently, we have reviewed a variety of nonparametric example-based super-resolution models exploiting different types of machine learning algorithms. The broadest classification considers whether the examples are internal, that is, extracted from the input image, or external, that is, extracted from an external database. The main advantage of these example-based approaches is that the resulting models can be effectively applied for larger upscaling factors, with resolution gains beyond the $1.6\times$ upper bound in reconstruction-based methods, providing robustness even for complex scenes that cannot be correctly handled by multiframe models.

9.1.1 Internal Learning Methods

Internal learning methods have the advantage of implicit adaptivity thanks to the fact that examples are extracted from different scales of the input

Example-Based Super Resolution. http://dx.doi.org/10.1016/B978-0-12-809703-8.00009-5

image. The shortcoming is that, in general, they require iterative application for providing large upscaling factors. The source of this limitation is that the cross-scale self-similarity property in natural images degrades with large scale differences (Glasner et al., 2009). We have explored two big families of internal learning methods: those based on high-frequency transfer and those based on neighbor embedding.

High-Frequency Transfer
About the former, we have seen that, properly limiting the extents of the search windows for internal examples, cross-scale self-similarity can be relatively efficiently applied, despite the iterative nature (Freedman & Fattal, 2011; C.-Y. Yang et al., 2014). We have also seen that, taking into account some possible degradations, like aliasing or additive noise, these models can be robustly applied in a variety of scenarios (J. B. Huang et al., 2015; Salvador, Pérez-Pellitero, & Kochale, 2013; Salvador et al., 2014).

Neighbor Embedding
We have described two different types of neighbor embedding approaches. The first one, based purely on self-examples, requires iterative upscaling as in high-frequency transfer and enriches the nearest-neighbor selection by considering phase variations in the low-resolution part of the examples (an alternative way to extend the number of examples is the generation of several low-resolution versions of the input image with different downscaling factors). Generally, neighbor-embedding methods exploit the common constraint of sum-to-one weights for the nearest neighbors to ensure that the solution is constrained to lie in the subspace of the high-resolution examples (Chang et al., 2004; Türkan et al., 2012, 2013). Further extensions might go in the direction of video processing, for example, considering the incorporation of epitomes in super resolution (Cheung et al., 2005; Türkan et al., 2015).

The second neighbor-embedding approach, which bridges the gap between internal and external learning, shows how the sum-to-one constraint used by Chang et al. (2004) can also be relaxed leading to enhanced regression with large dictionaries or sets of examples (Bevilacqua et al., 2012). These methods can be employed with both internal and external dictionaries. The advantage of large, external dictionaries is that single-step super resolution is feasible even for large upscaling factors. However, the cost of obtaining relevant neighbors becomes dominant unless fast nearest neighbor searches are employed (Barnes et al., 2009, 2010; He & Sun, 2012; McNames, 2001; Torres et al., 2014).

9.1.2 External Learning Methods

The most relevant research aspect in external learning methods is that of ensuring generalization with offline-trained models that provide efficient inference pipelines. In this book we have explored four different machine learning approaches that can be effectively applied for external learning super resolution.

Sparse Coding

The first one, sparse coding, follows the principles of neighbor embedding with the additional constraint of a compact, optimized dictionary that provides robust nearest-neighbor decomposition (J. Yang et al., 2010). Further specialization can be achieved by selecting training images that are more representative of the input image and compute a compact dictionary just in time (Pérez-Pellitero et al., 2013). This method enables effective super resolution for multiview scenarios, even if the camera rig is not calibrated, but introduces a higher computational cost due to the per-image dictionary training. In video applications, dictionaries can be periodically updated, exploiting the temporal correlation of video data. In any case, the optimization leading to the sparse decomposition of each patch is still a costly operation, even if using efficient approximation algorithms (Cai & Wang, 2011; Zeyde et al., 2012).

Anchored Regression

The second approach, anchored regression, builds on sparse coding and simplifies the problem by removing the sparsity constraint from the inference stage. In a baseline configuration directly emulating sparse coding, a linear regression matrix is anchored to each atom in the sparse optimized dictionary. Each regression matrix is built by using the high and low-resolution parts of the most similar atoms within the dictionary (Timofte et al., 2013). The simplified inference pipeline consists in looking for the nearest neighbor within the compact dictionary and applying the corresponding regression matrix. A further improvement of this model comes from the use of all training examples for computing the regression matrices (Pérez-Pellitero et al., 2014; Timofte et al., 2014) and efficient anchor search schemes, for example, based on hashing (Pérez-Pellitero et al., 2014) for efficient inference.

Random Forests

A more unifying framework that enables effective learning and fast inference is provided by regression trees and forests (J.-J. Huang et al., 2015; Schulter et al., 2015). In order to provide better generalization and keep efficiency, it is beneficial to exploit an ensemble with several randomized regression trees. The downside is the increased cost induced by fetching and applying the regression matrices for all trees in the ensemble. In order to work around this problem, we have also reviewed a mechanism for selecting the single tree in the ensemble that provides an accuracy similar to that of applying the entire ensemble, but with the advantage of a reduced cost for the linear regression stage (Salvador & Pérez-Pellitero, 2015). Further cost reductions can be reached through better understanding of the underlying low-resolution patch manifold structure (Pérez-Pellitero, Salvador, Ruiz-Hidalgo, & Rosenhahn, 2016a, 2016b, 2016c). The selection of the optimal representation of the visual data remains an open question for this and all the former approaches.

Deep Learning

This framework allows end-to-end optimization of hierarchical data representations, thus implicitly solving the problem of optimal feature representation. Even though the running time might be higher than in the highly streamlined random forests and the training stage much more costly, deep learning methods offer state-of-the-art accuracy when the network design is carefully chosen. We have seen how generic convolutional networks can be effective even with relatively thin networks (Dong et al., 2014), and also that the additional computational power (and running time) resulting from enlarging the extents of the spatial interactions in the network can improve the reconstruction accuracy (Dong et al., 2016). Most interestingly, the introduction of domain knowledge in the network design allows for further improvement of the reconstruction accuracy, reducing the number of parameters to be learned and, consequently, simplifying the training process (Z. Wang et al., 2015).

9.2 PERSPECTIVE

Recently, the accuracy and efficiency of super-resolution methods based on machine learning have reached a point where, using current computational resources, high-quality upscaling can already be deployed for many applications. The selection of the best suited algorithmic approach must consider several aspects. One of them is whether a specific image prior for the application exists, for example, industrial supervision of manufactured pieces, or medical imaging. We must also consider whether it is reasonable to apply external learning, as in terms of memory or generalization, or which level of computational complexity is allowed, for example, memory vs. running time vs. accuracy trade-off. In general, the answer to each problem will require a careful consideration of the constraints introduced by the application scenario. One of the goals of this book is to assist developers and researchers through the description of techniques that can be combined to further improve the fitting of known nonparametric example-based super-resolution methods to the specific requirements of each application.

One of the obvious applications fields for example-based super resolution is imaging. In the near future, it will be necessary to increase spatial resolution of existing audiovisual contents to match the resolution of the upcoming generations of ultra high-definition video, for example, 8K video, with a pixel count equivalent to 4 4K ultra high-definition frames or 16 high-definition ones. For these applications, which often run in embedded hardware, it is necessary to apply fast and efficient super-resolution methods, so forest-based methods are good candidates. Related applications include coding and transmission through bandwidth-limited channels (e.g., video over internet), postprocessing and editing pipelines (e.g., economic rendering of visual effects in high-definition resolution and posterior upscaling to target resolution, or legacy video restoration) and also visualization for entertainment (e.g., upscaling of computer graphics or depth images in gaming consoles or computers).

Light-field or plenoptic imaging is an interesting target application for super resolution. In this scenario, very low spatial resolution is natively available due to the use of a single image sensor to capture the light rays corresponding to different perspectives. In contrast with more general imaging problems, for example, video or uncalibrated multiview video, the registration between available perspectives in a light-field capture has a much higher precision (Ng, 2006). Further research on methods for combining the advantages of multiframe super resolution and example-based priors (Bätz et al., 2015) might provide the required level of quality and robustness for the use of light-field imaging in professional applications without requiring the presence of additional cameras to compensate for the low spatial resolution (Boominathan, Mitra, & Veeraraghavan, 2014). Other application fields involve the combination of super resolution with other tasks. For example, it might be of interest to jointly upscale the temporal and spatial resolution of video sequences (Salvador, Kochale, & Schweidler, 2013; Shahar et al., 2011). Another upcoming trend in imaging is high-dynamic range (HDR) imaging. HDR is often achieved through the fusion of images of the same scene captured with different exposures (Rubinstein, 2004). The application of super resolution to this scenario aims at jointly fusing the multiple exposures and enhancing the resolution of images (Ma & Wang, 2015; Traonmilin & Aguerrebere, 2014).

The bottom line is that, despite the improvements introduced by the latest nonparametric image models, which are in turn based on tuned state-of-the-art machine learning methods, the application of super resolution to specific problems still requires the careful selection of suitable algorithms and representations based on domain knowledge of the target task. Hopefully, the reader will now be able to independently evaluate, select, and improve existing super-resolution methods by analyzing the capabilities of current approaches and understanding the expectations of future ones. Of special interest, due to the sparse amount of available methods, is the problem of combining reconstruction-based and example-based super resolution. Further research in this direction might provide extended performance for related problems such as super resolution for light-field imaging, joint HDR imaging and upscaling and super resolution for general video sequences or multiview setups.

REFERENCES

Aharon, M., Elad, M., & Bruckstein, A. (2006). K-SVD: an algorithm for designing overcomplete dictionaries for sparse representation. *IEEE Transactions on Signal Processing, 54*(11), 4311–4322.

Arbelaez, P., Maire, M., Fowlkes, C., & Malik, J. (2011). Contour detection and hierarchical image segmentation. *IEEE Transactions on Pattern Analysis and Machine Intelligence, 33*(5), 898–916.

Baker, S., & Kanade, T. (2002). Limits on super-resolution and how to break them. *IEEE Transactions on Pattern Analysis and Machine Intelligence, 24*(9), 1167–1183.

Baker, S., Scharstein, D., Lewis, J. P., Roth, S., Black, M. J., & Szeliski, R. (2011). A database and evaluation methodology for optical flow. *International Journal of Computer Vision, 92*, 1–31.

Barnes, C., Shechtman, E., Finkelstein, A., & Goldman, D. B. (2009). PatchMatch: a randomized correspondence algorithm for structural image editing. *ACM Transactions on Graphics (Proceedings of SIGGRAPH), 28*(3).

Barnes, C., Shechtman, E., Goldman, D. B., & Finkelstein, A. (2010). The generalized patchmatch correspondence algorithm. In *Proceedings of the European conference on computer vision: Part III* (p. 29–43).

Bätz, M., Eichenseer, A., Seiler, J., Jonscher, M., & Kaup, A. (2015). Hybrid super-resolution combining example-based single-image and interpolation-based multi-image reconstruction approaches. In *Proceedings of IEEE international conference on image processing* (p. 58–62).

Bengio, Y., Lamblin, P., Popovici, D., & Larochelle, H. (2007). Greedy layer-wise training of deep networks. In *Proceedings of neural information processing systems.*

Bernard, S., Heutte, L., & Adam, S. (2009). On the selection of decision trees in random forests. In *Proceedings of the international joint conference on neural networks* (p. 302–307).

Bevilacqua, M., Roumy, A., Guillemot, C., & Alberi-Morel, M.-L. (2012). Low-complexity single-image super-resolution based on nonnegative neighbor embedding. In *Proceedings of the British machine vision conference* (p. 1–10).

Boiman, O., Shechtman, E., & Irani, M. (2008). In defense of nearest-neighbor based image classification. In *Proceedings of IEEE conference on computer vision and pattern recognition* (p. 1–8).

Boominathan, V., Mitra, K., & Veeraraghavan, A. (2014). Improving resolution and depth-of-field of light field cameras using a hybrid imaging system. In *Proceedings of IEEE international conference on computational photography* (p. 1–10).

Breiman, L. (2001). Random forests. *Machine Learning, 45*(1), 5–32.

Buades, A., Coll, B., & Morel, J.-M. (2005). A non-local algorithm for image denoising. In *Proceedings of IEEE conference on computer vision and pattern recognition* (Vol. 2, p. 60–65).

Burger, H. C., Schuler, C. J., & Harmeling, S. (2012). Image denoising: can plain neural networks compete with BM3D? In *Proceedings of IEEE conference on computer vision and pattern recognition* (p. 4321–4328).

Cai, T. T., & Wang, L. (2011). Orthogonal matching pursuit for sparse signal recovery with noise. *IEEE Transactions on Information Theory, 57*(7), 4680–4688.

Chambolle, A. (2004). An algorithm for total variation minimization and applications. *Journal of Mathematical Imaging and Vision, 20*(1–2), 89–97.

Chang, H., Yeung, D.-Y., & Xiong, Y. (2004). Super-resolution through neighbor embedding. In *Proceedings of IEEE conference on computer vision and pattern recognition.*

Chaudhuri, S., & Manjunath, J. (2005). *Motion-free super-resolution*. New York: Springer-Verlag New York, Inc.

Cheung, V., Frey, B. J., & Jojic, N. (2005). Video epitomes. In *Proceedings of IEEE conference on computer vision and pattern recognition* (Vol. 1, p. 42–49).

Criminisi, A., Shotton, J., & Konukoglu, E. (2011). Decision forests: a unified framework for classification, regression, density estimation, manifold learning and semi-supervised learning. *Foundations and Trends in Computer Graphics and Vision*,(7), 81–227.

Cui, Z., Chang, H., Shan, S., Zhong, B., & Chen, X. (2014). Deep network cascade for image super-resolution. In D. Fleet, T. Pajdla, B. Schiele, & T. Tuytelaars (Eds.), *Computer vision—ECCV 2014: 13th European conference, Zurich, Switzerland, September 6–12, 2014, Proceedings, Part V* (p. 49–64). Berlin: Springer International Publishing.

Dabov, K., Foi, A., Katkovnik, V., & Egiazarian, K. (2007). Image denoising by sparse 3-D transform-domain collaborative filtering. *IEEE Transactions on Image Processing, 16*(8), 2080–2095.

Dabov, K., Foi, A., Katkovnik, V., & Egiazarian, K. (2008). Image restoration by sparse 3D transform-domain collaborative filtering. In *Proceedings of the society of photo-optical instrumentation engineers* (Vol. 6812, p. 6).

Dai, D., Wang, Y., Chen, Y., & Van Gool, L. (2016). Is image super-resolution helpful for other vision tasks? In *Proceeding of IEEE winter conference on applications of computer vision*.

Daubechies, I., Defrise, M., & DeMol, C. (2004). An iterative thresholding algorithm for linear inverse problems with a sparsity constraint. *Communications on Pure and Applied Mathematics, 57*, 1413–1541.

Dempster, A. P., Laird, N. M., & Rubin, D. B. (1977). Maximum likelihood from incomplete data via the EM algorithm. *Journal of the Royal Statistical Society, Series B, 39*(1), 1–38.

Dong, C., Loy, C. C., He, K., & Tang, X. (2014). Learning a deep convolutional network for image super-resolution. In *Proceeding of the European conference on computer vision* (p. 184–199).

Dong, C., Loy, C. C., He, K., & Tang, X. (2016). Image super-resolution using deep convolutional networks. *IEEE Transactions on Pattern Analysis and Machine Intelligence, 38*(2), 295–307.

Eggermont, P. P. B. (1993). Maximum entropy regularization for Fredholm integral equations of the first kind. *SIAM Journal on Mathematical Analysis, 24*(6), 1557–1576.

Eigen, D., Krishnan, D., & Fergus, R. (2013). *Restoring an image taken through a window covered with dirt or rain*. In *Proceedings of the IEEE international conference on computer vision* (p. 633–640).

Elad, M., & Datsenko, D. (2009). Example-based regularization deployed to super-resolution reconstruction of a single image. *The Computer Journal, 52*(1), 15–30.

Farsiu, S., Robinson, M. D., Elad, M., & Milanfar, P. (2003). Fast and robust super-resolution. In *Proceedings of IEEE international conference on image processing* (Vol. 3, p. 291–294).

Farsiu, S., Robinson, M. D., Elad, M., & Milanfar, P. (2004). Fast and robust multiframe super resolution. *IEEE Transactions on Image Processing, 13*(10), 1327–1344.

Fattal, R. (2007). Image upsampling via imposed edge statistics. *ACM Transactions on Graphics*, (26), 3.

Fisher, R. (1953). Dispersion on a sphere. In *Proceedings of the Royal Society of London. Mathematical and physical sciences*.

Freedman, G., & Fattal, R. (2011). Image and video upscaling from local self-examples. *ACM Transactions on Graphics, 30*(2), 12:1–12:11.

Freeman, W. T., Jones, T. R., & Pasztor, E. C. (2002). Example-based super-resolution. *IEEE Computer Graphics and Applications, 22*(2), 56–65.

Freeman, W. T., Pasztor, E. C., & Carmichael, O. T. (2000). Learning low-level vision. *International Journal on Computer Vision, 40*(1), 25–47.

Freund, Y., Dasgupta, S., Kabra, M., & Verma, N. (2007). Learning the structure of manifolds using random projections. In *Proceedings of neural information processing systems*.

Gao, X., Zhang, K., Tao, D., & Li, X. (2012). Image super-resolution with sparse neighbor embedding. *IEEE Transactions on Image Processing, 21*(7), 3194–3205.

Glasner, D., Bagon, S., & Irani, M. (2009). Super-resolution from a single image. In *Proceedings of the international conference on computer vision* (p. 349–356).

Glorot, X., Bordes, A., & Bengio, Y. (2011). Deep sparse rectifier neural networks. In *Proceedings of the international conference on artificial intelligence and statistics* (p. 315–323).

Goldluecke, B., & Cremers, D. (2011). Introducing total curvature for image processing. In *Proceedings of IEEE international conference on computer vision* (p. 1267–1274).

Green, P. J. (1984). Iteratively reweighted least squares for maximum likelihood estimation, and some robust and resistant alternatives. *Journal of the Royal Statistical Society, Series B, 46*(2), 149–192.

Gregor, K., & LeCun, Y. (2010). Learning fast approximations of sparse coding. In *Proceedings of the international conference on machine learning* (p. 399–406).

Gupta, M. R., & Chen, Y. (2011). Theory and use of the EM algorithm. *Foundations and Trends in Computer Graphics and Vision, 4*(3), 223–296.

Hanson, R. J., & Lawson, C. L. (1974). *Solving least squares problems*. Englewood Cliffs, NJ: Prentice-Hall.

He, K., & Sun, J. (2012). Computing nearest-neighbor fields via propagation-assisted KD-trees. In *Proceedings of IEEE conference on computer vision and pattern recognition* (p. 111–118).

Heo, J.-P., Lee, Y. W., He, J., Chang, S.-F., & Yoon, S. (2012). Spherical hashing. In *Proceedings of IEEE conference on computer vision and pattern recognition*.

Hinton, G. E., & Salkhutdinov, R. R. (2006). Reducing the dimensionality of data with neural networks. *Science, 313*, 504–507.

Horn, B. K. P., & Schunck, B. G. (1981). Determining optical flow. *Artificial Intelligence, 17*, 185–203.

Huang, J. B., Singh, A., & Ahuja, N. (2015). Single image super-resolution from transformed self-exemplars. In *Proceedings of IEEE conference on computer vision and pattern recognition* (p. 5197–5206).

Huang, J.-J., Siu, W.-C., & Liu, T.-R. (2015). Fast image interpolation via random forests. *IEEE Transactions on Image Processing, 24*(10), 3232–3245.

Huang, T. S., & Tsai, R. Y. (1984). Multiple frame image restoration and registration. In *Proceedings of advances in computer vision and image processing* (p. 317–339).

Indyk, P., & Motwani, R. (1998). Approximate nearest neighbors: towards removing the curse of dimensionality. In *Proceedings of the ACM symposium on theory of computing* (p. 604–613).

Irani, M., & Peleg, S. (1990). Super resolution from image sequences. In *Proceedings of the international conference on pattern recognition* (Vol. 2, p. 115–120).

Irani, M., & Peleg, S. (1991). Improving resolution by image registration. *Graphical Models and Image Processing, 53*(3), 231–239.

Jain, V., & Seung, H. S. (2008). Natural image denoising with convolutional networks. In *Proceedings of neural information processing systems*.

Jojic, N., Frey, B. J., & Kannan, A. (2003). Epitomic analysis of appearance and shape. In *Proceedings of IEEE international conference on computer vision* (Vol. 1, p. 34–41).

Joshi, N., Szeliski, R., & Kriegman, D. J. (2008). PSF estimation using sharp edge prediction. In *Proceedings of IEEE conference on computer vision and pattern recognition* (p. 1–8).

Kim, K. I., & Kwon, Y. (2010). Single-image super-resolution using sparse regression and natural image prior. *IEEE Transactions on Pattern Analysis and Machine Intelligence, 32*(6), 1127–1133.

Kim, S. P., Bose, N. K., & Valenzuela, H. M. (1990). Recursive reconstruction of high resolution image from noisy undersampled multiframes. *IEEE Transactions on Acoustics, Speech, and Signal Processing, 38*(6), 1013–1027.

Korman, S., & Avidan, S. (2011). Coherency sensitive hashing. In *Proceedings of the international conference on computer vision* (p. 1607–1614).

Krizhevsky, A., Sutskever, I., & Hinton, G. E. (2012). ImageNet classification with deep convolutional neural networks. In *Proceedings of neural information processing systems.*

Krüger, N., Janssen, P., Kalkan, S., Lappe, M., Leonardis, A., Piater, J., ... Wiskott, L. (2013). Deep hierarchies in the primate visual cortex: what can we learn for computer vision? *IEEE Transactions on Pattern Analysis and Machine Intelligence, 35*(8), 1847–1871.

Lawson, C. L., & Hanson, R. J. (1974). Solving least squares problems. Englewood Cliffs, NJ: Prentice-Hall.

LeCun, Y., Boser, B., Denker, J. S., Henderson, D., Howard, R. E., Hubbard, W., & Jackel, L. D. (1989). Backpropagation applied to handwritten zip code recognition. *Neural Computation, 1*(4), 541–551.

Lee, H., Battle, A., Raina, R., & Ng, A. Y. (2007). Efficient sparse coding algorithms. In *Proceedings of neural information processing systems* (p. 801–808).

Li, X., & Orchard, M. T. (2001). New edge-directed interpolation. *IEEE Transactions on Image Processing, 10*(10), 1521–1527.

Lin, Y., Chen, H. H., Jiang, Z. H., & Hsai, H. F. (2004). Image resizing with raised cosine pulses. In *Proceedings of international symposium on intelligent signal processing and communication systems* (p. 581–585).

Lin, Z., & Shum, H.-Y. (2004). Fundamental limits of reconstruction-based superresolution algorithms under local translation. *IEEE Transactions on Pattern Analysis and Machine Intelligence, 26*(1), 83–97.

Liu, C., & Sun, D. (2014). On Bayesian adaptive video super resolution. *IEEE Transactions on Pattern Analysis and Machine Intelligence, 36*(2), 346–360.

Liu, X., Tanaka, M., & Okutomi, M. (2012). Noise level estimation using weak textured patches of a single noisy image. In *Proceedings of IEEE international conference on image processing* (p. 665–668).

Lloyd, S. (1982). Least squares quantization in PCM. *IEEE Transactions on Information Theory, 28*(2), 129–137.

Lowe, D. G. (2004). Distinctive image features from scale-invariant keypoints. *International Journal on Computer Vision, 60*(2), 91–110.

Lu, X., Yuan, H., Yan, P., Yuan, Y., & Li, X. (2012). Geometry constrained sparse coding for single image super-resolution. In *Proceedings of IEEE conference on computer vision and pattern recognition* (p. 1648–1655).

Lucas, B. D., & Kanade, T. (1981). An iterative image registration technique with an application to stereo vision. In *Proceedings of the international joint conference on artificial intelligence* (p. 674–679).

Ma, K., & Wang, Z. (2015). Multi-exposure image fusion: a patch-wise approach. In *Proceedings of IEEE international conference on image processing* (p. 1717–1721).

McCann, S., & Lowe, D. G. (2012). Local Naive Bayes Nearest Neighbor for image classification. In *Proceedings of IEEE conference on computer vision and pattern recognition* (p. 3650–3656).

McNames, J. (2001). A fast nearest neighbor algorithm based on a principal axis search tree. *IEEE Transactions on Pattern Analysis and Machine Intelligence, 23*(9), 964–976.

Michaeli, T., & Irani, M. (2013). Nonparametric blind super-resolution. In *Proceedings of IEEE international conference on computer vision* (p. 945–952).

Nair, V., & Hinton, G. E. (2010). Rectified linear units improve restricted Boltzmann machines. In *Proceedings of the international conference on machine learning* (p. 807–814).

Ng, R. (2006). *Digital light field photography* (Unpublished doctoral dissertation). Stanford University.

Pantin, E., & Starck, J.-l. (1996). Deconvolution of astronomical images using the multiscale maximum entropy method. *Astronomy and Astrophysics, Supplement Series, 315*, 31–35.

Park, S. C., Park, M. K., & Kang, M. G. (2003). Super-resolution image reconstruction: a technical overview. *IEEE Signal Processing Magazine, 20*(3), 21–36.

Pérez-Pellitero, E., Salvador, J., Ruiz-Hidalgo, J., & Rosenhahn, B. (2013). Bayesian region selection for adaptive dictionary-based super-resolution. In *Proceedings of the British machine vision conference*.

Pérez-Pellitero, E., Salvador, J., Ruiz-Hidalgo, J., & Rosenhahn, B. (2016a). Antipodally invariant metrics for fast regression-based super-resolution. *IEEE Transactions on Image Processing, 25*(6), 2456–2468.

Pérez-Pellitero, E., Salvador, J., Ruiz-Hidalgo, J., & Rosenhahn, B. (2016b). Half hypersphere confinement for piecewise linear regression. In *Proceedings of IEEE winter conference on applications of computer vision*.

Pérez-Pellitero, E., Salvador, J., Ruiz-Hidalgo, J., & Rosenhahn, B. (2016c). PSyCo: manifold span reduction for super resolution. In *Proceedings of IEEE conference on computer vision and pattern recognition*.

Pérez-Pellitero, E., Salvador, J., Torres, I., Ruiz-Hidalgo, J., & Rosenhahn, B. (2014). Fast super-resolution via dense local training and inverse regressor search. In *Proceedings of Asian conference on computer vision*.

Peyré, G. (2009). Manifold models for signals and images. *Computer Vision and Image Understanding, 113*(2), 249–260.

Pickup, L. C., Capel, D. P., Roberts, S. J., & Zisserman, A. (2007). Overcoming registration uncertainty in image super-resolution: maximize or marginalize? *EURASIP Journal on Advances in Signal Processing, 2007*, Article ID 2356.

Revaud, J., Weinzaepfel, P., Harchaoui, Z., & Schmid, C. (2015). EpicFlow: edge-preserving interpolation of correspondences for optical flow. In *Proceedings of IEEE conference on computer vision and pattern recognition*.

Roweis, S. T., & Saul, L. K. (2000). Nonlinear dimensionality reduction by locally linear embedding. *Science, 290*(5500), 2323–2326.

Rubinstein, R. (2004). *Fusion of differently exposed image sequences* (Tech. Rep.). Technion.

Rudin, L. I., Osher, S., & Fatemi, E. (1992). Nonlinear total variation based noise removal algorithms. *Physica D, 60*(1–4), 259–268.

Rumelhart, D. E., Hinton, G. E., & Williams, R. J. (1988). Learning representations by back-propagating errors. In Anderson, J. A. and Rosenfeld, E. (Ed.), *Neurocomputing: foundations of research* (p. 696–699). Cambridge, MA, USA: MIT Press.

Salvador, J., Kochale, A., & Schweidler, S. (2013). Patch-based spatio-temporal super-resolution for video with non-rigid motion. *Elsevier Signal Processing: Image Communication, 28*(5), 483–493.

Salvador, J., & Pérez-Pellitero, E. (2015). Naive Bayes Super-Resolution Forest. In *Proceedings of IEEE international conference on computer vision* (p. 325–333).

Salvador, J., Pérez-Pellitero, E., & Kochale, A. (2013). Fast single-image super-resolution with filter selection. In *Proceedings of IEEE international conference on image processing* (p. 640–644).

Salvador, J., Pérez-Pellitero, E., & Kochale, A. (2014). Robust single-image super-resolution using cross-scale self-similarity. In *Proceedings of IEEE international conference on image processing* (p. 2135–2139).

Schuler, C. J., Burger, H. C., Harmeling, S., & Schölkopf, B. (2013). A machine learning approach for non-blind image deconvolution. In *Proceedings of IEEE conference on computer vision and pattern recognition* (p. 1067–1074).

Schulter, S., Leistner, C., & Bischof, H. (2015). Fast and accurate image upscaling with super-resolution forests. In *Proceedings of IEEE conference on computer vision and pattern recognition*.

Shahar, O., Faktor, A., & Irani, M. (2011). Space-time super-resolution from a single video. In *Proceedings of IEEE conference on computer vision and pattern recognition* (p. 3353–3360).

Sheikh, H. R., Bovik, A. C., & de Veciana, G. (2005). An information fidelity criterion for image quality assessment using natural scene statistics. *IEEE Transactions on Image Processing, 14*(12), 2117–2128.

Singh, A., Porikli, F., & Ahuja, N. (2014). Super-resolving noisy images. In *Proceedings of IEEE conference on computer vision and pattern recognition* (p. 2846–2853).

Stark, H., & Oskoui, P. (1989). High-resolution image recovery from image-plane arrays, using convex projections. *Journal of the Optical Society of America. A, 6*(11), 1715–1726.

Sun, D., Roth, S., & Black, M. J. (2010). Secrets of optical flow estimation and their principles. In *Proceedings of IEEE conference on computer vision and pattern recognition* (p. 2432–2439).

Sun, J., Zheng, N., Tao, H., & Shum, H. (2003). Image hallucination with primal sketch priors. In *Proceedings of IEEE conference on computer vision and pattern recognition* (Vol. 2, p. 729–736).

Takeda, H., Farsiu, S., & Milanfar, P. (2008). Deblurring using regularized locally adaptive kernel regression. *IEEE Transactions on Image Processing, 17*(4), 550–563.

Tappen, M. F., Russell, B. C., & Freeman, W. T. (2003). Exploiting the sparse derivative prior for super-resolution and image demosaicing. In *Proceedings of IEEE workshop on statistical and computational theories of vision*.

Tikhonov, A. N., & Arsenin, V. Y. (1977). *Solutions of ill-posed problems*. Washington: W.H. Winston.

Timofte, R., De Smet, V., & Van Gool, L. (2013). Anchored neighborhood regression for fast example-based super-resolution. In *Proceedings of IEEE international conference on computer vision* (p. 1920–1927).

Timofte, R., De Smet, V., & Van Gool, L. (2014). A+: adjusted anchored neighborhood regression for fast super-resolution. In *Proceedings of Asian conference on computer vision*.

Timofte, R., Rothe, R., & Van Gool, L. (2016). Seven ways to improve example-based single image super resolution. In *Proceedings of IEEE conference on computer vision and pattern recognition*.

Tom, B. C., Katsaggelos, A. K., & Galatsanos, N. P. (1994). Reconstruction of a high resolution image from registration and restoration of low resolution images. In *Proceedings of IEEE international conference on image processing* (Vol. 3, p. 553–557).

Torres, I., Salvador, J., & Pérez-Pellitero, E. (2014). Fast approximate nearest-neighbor field by cascaded spherical hashing. In *Proceedings of Asian conference on computer vision*.

Traonmilin, Y., & Aguerrebere, C. (2014). Simultaneous high dynamic range and superresolution imaging without regularization. *SIAM Journal on Imaging Sciences, 7*(3), 1624–1644.

Tropp, J. A., & Gilbert, A. C. (2007). Signal recovery from random measurements via orthogonal matching pursuit. *IEEE Transactions on Information Theory, 53*(12), 4655–4666.

Tsai, R., & Huang, T. (1984). Multiframe image restoration and registration. In *Proceedings of advances in computer vision and image processing*.

Türkan, M., Alain, M., Thoreau, D., Guillotel, P., & Guillemot, C. (2015). Epitomic image factorization via neighbor-embedding. In *Proceedings of IEEE international conference on image processing* (p. 4141–4145).

Türkan, M., Thoreau, D., & Guillotel, P. (2012). Self-content super-resolution for ultra-HD up-sampling. In *Proceeding of the European conference on visual media production* (p. 49–58).

Türkan, M., Thoreau, D., & Guillotel, P. (2013). Optimized neighbor embeddings for single-image super-resolution. In *Proceedings of IEEE international conference on image processing* (p. 645–649).

Türkan, M., Thoreau, D., & Guillotel, P. (2014). Iterated neighbor-embeddings for image super-resolution. In *Proceedings of IEEE international conference on image processing* (p. 3887–3891).

Vandewalle, P., Süsstrunk, S., & Vetterli, M. (2006). A frequency domain approach to registration of aliased images with application to super-resolution. *EURASIP Journal on Applied Signal Processing, 2006*, 233.

Wang, J., Kumar, S., & Chang, S.-F. (2010). Semi-supervised hashing for scalable image retrieval. In *Proceedings of IEEE conference on computer vision and pattern recognition*.

Wang, Z., Bovik, A. C., Sheikh, H. R., & Simoncelli, E. P. (2004). Image quality assessment: from error visibility to structural similarity. *IEEE Transactions on Image Processing, 13*(4), 600–612.

Wang, Z., Liu, D., Yang, J., Han, W., & Huang, T. (2015). Deep networks for image super-resolution with sparse prior. In *Proceedings of IEEE international conference on computer vision* (p. 370–378).

Weiss, Y., Torralba, A., & Fergus, R. (2008). Spectral hashing. In *Proceedings of neural information processing systems*.

Yang, C.-Y., Ma, C., & Yang, M.-H. (2014). Single-image super-resolution: a benchmark. In *Proceeding of the European conference on computer vision*.

Yang, C.-Y., & Yang, M.-H. (2013). Fast direct super-resolution by simple functions. In *Proceedings of IEEE international conference on computer vision* (p. 561–568).

Yang, J., Lin, Z., & Cohen, S. (2013). Fast image super-resolution based on in-place example regression. In *Proceedings of IEEE conference on computer vision and pattern recognition* (p. 1059–1066).

Yang, J., Wright, J., Huang, T., & Ma, Y. (2008). Image super-resolution as sparse representation of raw image patches. In *Proceedings of IEEE conference on computer vision and pattern recognition* (p. 1–8).

Yang, J., Wright, J., Huang, T. S., & Ma, Y. (2010). Image super-resolution via sparse representation. *IEEE Transactions on Image Processing, 19*(11), 2861–2873.

Zeyde, R., Elad, M., & Protter, M. (2012). On single image scale-up using sparse-representations. In *Proceedings of the international conference on curves and surfaces* (p. 711–730).

Zhang, K., Gao, X., Tao, D., & Li, X. (2012). Multi-scale dictionary for single image super-resolution. In *Proceedings of IEEE conference on computer vision and pattern recognition* (p. 1114–1121).

Zontak, M., Mosseri, I., & Irani, M. (2013). Separating signal from noise using patch recurrence across scales. In *Proceedings of IEEE conference on computer vision and pattern recognition* (p. 1195–1202).

Printed in the United States
By Bookmasters